THE ——— COMMUNICATION MOVEMENT

Unify Your People with the
Shared Language of Success

ERIK THERWANGER

BALBOA.PRESS

A DIVISION OF HAY HOUSE

This book is a work of non-fiction. Unless otherwise noted, the author and the publisher make no explicit guarantees as to the accuracy of the information contained in this book and in some cases, names of people and places have been altered to protect their privacy.

Balboa Press books may be ordered through booksellers or by contacting:

Balboa Press
A Division of Hay House
1663 Liberty Drive
Bloomington, IN 47403
www.balboapress.com
844-682-1282

Because of the dynamic nature of the Internet, any web addresses or links contained in this book may have changed since publication and may no longer be valid. The views expressed in this work are solely those of the author and do not necessarily reflect the views of the publisher, and the publisher hereby disclaims any responsibility for them.

The author of this book does not dispense medical advice or prescribe the use of any technique as a form of treatment for physical, emotional, or medical problems without the advice of a physician, either directly or indirectly. The intent of the author is only to offer information of a general nature to help you in your quest for emotional and spiritual well-being. In the event you use any of the information in this book for yourself, which is your constitutional right, the author and the publisher assume no responsibility for your actions.

Any people depicted in stock imagery provided by Getty Images are models, and such images are being used for illustrative purposes only. Certain stock imagery © Getty Images.

Print information available on the last page.

ISBN: 978-1-9822-5901-3 (sc)
ISBN: 978-1-9822-5900-6 (hc)
ISBN: 978-1-9822-5902-0 (e)

Library of Congress Control Number: 2020922832

Balboa Press rev. date: 12/21/2020

Dedication

This book is dedicated to every business leader, business professional, and individual who cares enough about their people to strive for team unification and wants to achieve greater results by becoming fluent in the *Shared Language of Success*.

To every client I have had the privilege of working with. You opened your doors and allowed me to start *The COMMUNICATION Movement* and unify your people. Your desire to create higher levels of team cohesion inspires me.

Contents

3
PILLARS OF BUSINESS
GREATNESS
LEADING
PLANNING
SELLING
ThinkGREAT

The 3 Pillars

Supporting Your Growth

Build - Strengthen - Expand

No matter what industry you are in, your organization is supported by three distinct disciplines that I call *pillars* – leadership development, strategic planning, and sales performance. A structural break, in any single pillar, can significantly impact your ability to fulfill your mission and achieve your vision.

The 3 Pillars of Business Greatness provide you with the resources to unify all three, increasing their strength and providing the support and cohesion necessary to exceed your goals. Unique to the business world, Think GREAT's three essential systems unify your people with a shared dialogue and create the greatest levels of structure, synergy, and success.

Developing your leaders, creating your strategic plan, and enhancing your sales system should not be taken lightly. Each book, *The LEADERSHIP Connection*, *ELEVATE*, and *Dynamic Sales COMBUSTION* forms a collective cohesion of strategies and techniques for greater results.

Welcome to The *COMMUNICATION Movement*.

The COMMUNICATION Movement will introduce you and your team to a revolutionary new way of communicating, one that focuses on creating the highest levels of identity, clarity, and teamwork, while simultaneously unifying your people and improving the results of your organization.

It's time to get everyone speaking the same language and collapse the time frames to reach excellence. You will no longer be limited to generic words and overused clichés. Now, you and your team will transform your destiny by increasing the power of each pillar while becoming fluent in the shared language of business champions.

Introduction

Make the Decision to Unify

Communication is Much More than Talking.

The early 1980s was filled with an explosion of musical styles – a different flavor for everyone. Sure, there were one-hit wonders but there were also bands, new and old, that dominated the radio stations. Moving the dial on your radio from left to right, you could hear the music of Duran Duran and Devo, Van Halen and Def Leopard, Run DMC and the Beastie Boys, The Go-Go's and Pat Benetar. What an era!

Just like every other teenager, I was into my music and loved the new sounds hitting the airwaves. I remember when my dad bought tickets for a "concert," promising a live performance that we would never forget. He said it would be a surprise and I was left wondering which band we would see. I was energized as we arrived at the Pantages Theatre in Los Angeles, California until I looked at the marquee... *The King and I*. Wait, what? A play?

Starring the late Yul Brynner, I was less than enthusiastic about seeing this "concert" and I am sure it showed on my face and it may have come out through my body language. My dad just kept saying, "Just give it a try." Since he drove us there, and we were about forty-five minutes from home, the best I could hope for was a decent concession stand.

As my dad led the way, my mom, brother, and I followed him to our seats. Stubbornly, I sat, certain that I would not enjoy it. As we waited for the show to start, it seemed like an eternity. In retrospect, it was probably only a half hour until the lights dimmed, the curtains opened, and the show began. The orchestra began to play music that was much different than anything heard on my radio. In my head, I remember saying, "I hate classical music."

The sweet harmonious sounds of each member of the orchestra began to set the tone in the auditorium. It was all perfectly timed, evoking the emotions of joy, sadness, humor, and passion. I found myself taken away, caught up in the performances of each actor, especially of Yul Brynner. By this date, he had performed this role over 4,000 times and when the show ended, he received a standing ovation from everyone, including me. What had happened? I was supposed to *not* like it.

Everything came together, so powerfully that even a teenager could appreciate it. The entire performance, from beginning to end, created a shared experience for everyone. During all of it, the orchestra masterfully performed the score, setting the tone that unified the whole audience, empowered every performer, and ultimately created the feeling, and the mood for the full show.

I went into the play with my arms crossed and my mind made up. But I emerged applauding, smiling, and filled with energy and excitement. The orchestra did not merely show up to do a job, they intentionally created a feeling that unified their audience – their customers. From the beginning of the show until the cast took their final bow, the orchestra maintained the sound that did more than fill our ears, it kept us in the moment and allowed us to experience the play, not just watch it.

Are some of your people just watching your business when they should be experiencing it? Are your customers merely observing it or are they enjoying the performance of your team? Thirty years later, I returned to my memories of that orchestra, and how they created a harmonious sound, so I could "compose the score" for greater results in business. My dad was right. I never forgot that performance and now, I teach leaders how to unify their teams as they learn to speak the same language – the *Shared Language of Success.*

DIALECT COACH

As a consultant for businesses, I have been referred to as a business coach, sales coach, leadership coach, personal coach, and corporate coach. But I consider myself a *dialect coach*. Yes, this is a self-appointed title but it represents the underlying focus of my coaching duties. I meet so many leaders who sum up their collective circumstances with their people as, "We are not speaking the same language."

So, I help business leaders, their teams, and individuals to have an enhanced dialect, an intentional way of communicating that fosters positivity and empowerment in everyone who experiences it – just like the orchestra did when I was a teenager.

As we glide through the pages of this book, I will elaborate on each of my experiences, from a variety of different industries, with their use of language in the workplace. But first, here's the "Cliff's Notes" version of my background, so you can understand my pathway to the title of dialect coach and the critical need for your business to infuse the *Shared Language of Success* into your culture.

My first full-time job began in 1987. I served in the United States Marine Corps as an air traffic controller. The Corps had a very distinctive language spoken by every member in their ranks but I was also taught to speak "aviation." After my tour of duty, I used my G.I. Bill to pursue a career in filmmaking, studying cinema, and television at the University of Southern California. Then, I began working at a post-production company in Santa Monica, which again used a specific language among its members.

I left the entertainment industry in 1999 when my new bride was diagnosed with cancer. While I was her caregiver, I started a new journey, selling financial services, and yet again, experienced their unique language. In 2003, I re-entered the media industry and worked my way up to become the vice president of another post-production company.

In 2009, I combined my experiences from three vastly different industries: military, media, and financial services, and I founded Think GREAT. I began my new career by coaching people on techniques to set and accomplish their goals – no matter what circumstances they faced. It did not take long for me to include business coaching and I began to work with sales professionals, leaders, and their team members.

I transformed into an author, speaker, and business consultant, sharing the techniques I created that helped me rise to the position of vice president and allowed a media company to achieve annual sales growth of over 300%. By 2017, I had thousands of hours of coaching under my belt and I began recognizing that the greatest results were linked to teams that were unified through the specific language I had introduced them to.

When people communicate in a unifying way, they form an unmatched synergy and they perform at the highest levels. Unfortunately, this language is often missing. To the credit of each organization I begin working with, their people are typically fluent in the language necessary to run their business but not "bilingual" with the language to effectively communicate with their people – their teams – the *Shared Language of Success.*

BUSINESS LANGUAGE

While each business has some form of a common language, it is usually limited to four specific areas – their company, their industry, their products, and their services.

Business Language – the collective use of words, phrases, gestures, and actions that are necessary for an understanding of the elements required for a business to <u>survive</u>. This language creates cohesion for a <u>business</u>.

Stepping into a bank, a restaurant, or a real estate office, one would expect people working in those businesses to "speak the language."

Examples of Business Language:

BANKING	RESTAURANT	REAL ESTATE
Checking Account	Sous-Chef	Title Insurance
Accrued Interest	Al dente	Foreclosure
Routing Number	Back of House	Open House
Money Market Fund	Medium Rare	Unsecured Loan
Certificate of Deposit (CD)	Dine and Dash	Accelerated Amortization

It would send up red flags if you wanted to buy a house and asked your realtor if there were any open houses you could see and she replied with, "What's an open house?" While most people are fluent in their *Business Language*, they are speechless when it comes time to speak the *Shared Language of Success* - the communication techniques that will unify their teams and significantly impact their businesses. But it's not their fault. Most don't even know this language exists.

According to Ethnologue, a publication that identifies known languages, in 2020, there were "7,117 languages" spoken throughout our world of 195 countries and over 7.8 billion people. There are also many different definitions of the word, *language*, so let's take a look at the two most prolific.

Lan · guage

noun

- the method of human communication, either spoken or written, consisting of the use of words in a structured and conventional way.
- a systematic means of communicating ideas or feelings by the use of conventionalized signs, sounds, gestures, or marks having understood meanings.

The first definition refers to the use of words for human communication but is limited in its scope. This definition aligns more with the *Business Language* spoken in most organizations – the unique words for their particular industry.

It is the second definition that begins to tap into the power of language - *communicating ideas or feelings.... understood meanings.* It is not limited to words but includes signs, sounds, and gestures. This definition aligns more with the *Shared Language of Business Success.*

Shared Language – the collective use of words, phrases, gestures, and actions that are necessary for an understanding of the elements required for a business to <u>thrive</u>. This language creates cohesion for your <u>people</u>.

The power of a shared language is undeniable and I will use the pages of this book to introduce you to examples of this phenomenon and the techniques that will unify everyone with the *Shared Language of Success.*

The COMMUNICATION Movement will position you and your team to achieve higher levels of success as everyone understands the deeper significance of:

1. The WORDS we choose
2. The SPEECHES we share
3. The GESTURES we make
4. The ACTIONS we take

Are you ready for the excitement, energy, passion, enthusiasm, and electric feeling of a team that operates in sync? If you answered yes, and I know you did, then you need to have everyone speaking the same language, being on the same page, singing the same song - you know all of the clichés. Now, it's time to learn how to transform clichés into powerful realities.

Everyone hears and observes everything in your organization. Leaders, team members, clients, customers, prospects, and vendors all analyze the language they experience, forming powerful opinions that impact every aspect of your business. When we fail to be aware of the language we are using, we fail to make the impact we are intending.

Whether my client is a small mom-and-pop shop, a medium-size charity organization, a large business, or a publicly-traded Fortune 500 company, everyone benefits when their teams do more than just speak their *Business Language. W*hen they become fluent in the *Shared Language of Success*, they trend their results upward. You are about to begin *The COMMUNICATION Movement* and provide purpose to the *language* used in your environment and experience the beautiful harmony of team cohesion.

Think GREAT,

Erik

DIALECT TUNING

Language Empowerment System (LES)

Communication works for those who work at it.

~ John Powell

Dialect Tuning

Language Empowerment System (LES)

Fine-Tuning Your Communication.

Orchestras can be comprised of many players and many instruments. Musical tuning is critical to the sound of each instrument as well as the shared sound of the entire orchestra. When two or more instruments play together it is important that they are in tune with each other. One instrument, improperly tuned, could be heard by the entire audience and have a dramatic impact on the desired emotional result of the collective performance.

Similarly, one team member, who fails to fine-tune their communication, could have a devastating impact on your entire team, company, and end-users. Worse yet, imagine the impact when multiple members of your team fail to speak the *Shared Language of Success*.

Tuning a musical instrument means preparing it to play at the correct pitch: not too high or too low. Untuned instruments produce sounds that create disturbances in the "flow" of the music. Musicians ensure that their instruments are properly tuned as a professional and common courtesy for the audience. Like a highly trained musician, people in the workplace must fine-tune their communication to avoid a disturbance in the "flow" of the message. This, too, is a professional and common courtesy.

While I don't read music, I understand that a symphony is made up of four distinct parts, all necessary for the collective effectiveness of the entire piece. The roots of the symphony can be traced back to the overtures of operas during the Baroque period, and by the late 17th century, thanks in part to Alessandro Scarlatti, symphonies started to take shape and were continually developed in the following decades.

Symphony parts, also known as *movements*, are typically free-standing, and when one movement ends, there is a pause, then the next movement begins. Each section is conceived as parts of a whole and they relate to one another. The German word for *Sentence* is *Satz* and is commonly used to refer to a movement in a musical piece. Hence the four parts, or movements, of a symphony are designed to fit together just as the four sentences of this paragraph are all linked together to create a deeper meaning and understanding of my intended message.

While some symphonies have three or five movements, with rare exceptions, most use a standardized pattern consisting of four movements to take the audience on an emotional journey. It is imperative that the conductor, and all members of the orchestra, understand each movement if they want to achieve their desired results while performing together.

Your business is no different. Leaders and team members must understand each movement involved in the *Shared Language of Success* and how to achieve the desired results while performing together. Just as every orchestra can play beautiful and moving music, when their instruments are tuned properly, every team can create a seamless harmony when everyone is speaking the same language of success and using properly tuned communication.

It would be easy to write a book about all the challenges we encounter in business. I hear the endless barrage of struggles, difficulties, and headaches that people face. Interestingly, one challenge seems to be shared by nearly everyone I coach – communication! If I had a nickel for every time I heard a leader say, "We are not speaking the same language," I could fix the United States budget deficit. Much deeper than referring to the misuse of the English language, they use this cliché to describe a void that exists.

Something is missing, and it can be felt. More than mere types of poor communication, like misleading, unclear, late, untimely, and irrelevant dialogue, they are referring to the lack of a language that unifies their people. When our people are not "speaking the same language" the impact can be significant, causing major problems, unnecessary mistakes, and unwanted disengagement that all could have been avoided with the proper tuning of our communication.

You will need more than just good intentions to harness the power of a unifying language. To unify your people, you must create a movement.

CREATING A MOVEMENT

Your team is far too important to leave their unification to chance or hope for the best. Just as an orchestra does much more than play music by following the four movements of a symphony, the *Language Empowerment System (LES)* will create a powerful cohesion in your people as they apply the four movements of the *Shared Language of Success*.

The Four Movements of a Symphony:

1. Fast Movement
2. Slow Movement
3. Dance Movement
4. Strong Movement

The Four Movements of the Shared Language of Success:

1. The WORDS we choose
2. The SPEECHES we share
3. The GESTURES we make
4. The ACTIONS we take

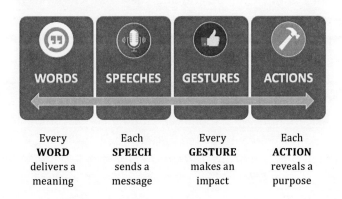

WORDS	SPEECHES	GESTURES	ACTIONS
Every **WORD** delivers a meaning	Each **SPEECH** sends a message	Every **GESTURE** makes an impact	Each **ACTION** reveals a purpose

The COMMUNICATION Movement is your language manual. But do not keep it hidden in a desk drawer. This unique tool is divided into four powerful sections and will guide you, step-by-step, to understand and improve each component of a cohesive language that unifies your entire team, enhances performance, and impacts everyone who experiences it.

Part I: The WORDS We Choose

Magnetize the impact of the words spoken in your workplace to ***Build Strong Identities*** that increase engagement levels. Team performance will elevate as your words ***Create Exceptional Attitudes*** in your people. Unifying everyone will position your organization to succeed and allow leaders to ***Assemble Remarkable Teams***.

Part II: The SPEECHES We Share

As we intentionally select powerful words to connect, we will discover that our ***Vocal Creations Influence*** and our ***Dialogue Inspires Activity*** in those who hear our new style of communication. Enthusiasm, engagement, and empowerment will spread like wildfire as our ***Phraseology Fosters Success*** throughout our entire organization.

Part III: The GESTURES We Make

Body language is part of everyday life and affects the business workplace but often in the wrong way. Discover that ***Nonverbal Cues Reveal Clues*** about your people and their ***Body Language Shapes Trust*** levels among everyone – inside and outside of your company. Most importantly, pay close attention because ***Physical Motions Foreshadow Actions***.

Part IV: The ACTIONS We Take

Without action, nothing happens, including the accomplishment of our goals. Complacency is not an option when success is desired, so we must focus on ***Synchronizing Our Performance*** while we are also ***Harmonizing Our Efforts***. To create the highest levels of teamwork, we must fully unify our people by ***Boosting Recognition***.

NEVER SETTLE FOR A KAZOO

The kazoo - you know you've played one. We all have. But it does not qualify us as musicians. It's regarded more like a toy than an actual instrument and has been known to create a shrill, obnoxious, and annoying sound that causes people to become quickly irritated. When our people fail to speak the *Shared Language of Success*, it's like a kazoo concert in our workplace environments.

When it comes to using a language that unifies people, does your current team communicate like an orchestra performing a symphony with fine-tuned instruments or do they sound like a bunch of novice kazoo players?

In the regard to communication that unites people, not just speaking our *Business Language*, most leaders and team members are speechless. Failing to speak the *Shared Language of Success*, increases the difficulty of any task, even the most basic. It is a costly endeavor and can waste both time and money while reducing team morale and your overall results.

The COMMUNICATION Movement will transform the words, speeches, gestures, and actions permeating your organization and convert them into a shared language that unifies your entire team and empowers them to hit the high notes required for success.

Throughout the pages of this book, you will fine-tune your communication with each *Sound Bite*, just like the one below. These tips, concepts, and insights will further enhance the harmony and impact of your message. At the end of each chapter, you will be able to use a *Communication Catalyst* – exercises to unify your team and further improve workplace communication.

 **Sound Bite:**
The *Shared Language of Success* is a unifying tool that brings people together and creates a cohesion of unmatched excellence.

COMMUNICATION TUNING

A friend excitedly told me, "I went to the symphony last night." What he was trying to say was that he went to hear an orchestra that happened to be playing a symphony. If he had said, "they played a moving symphony," then he would have been referring to the piece of music itself.

There is a difference between a symphony and an orchestra. But let's also acknowledge that there was one other critical word my friend left out that was necessary for the performance he experienced – conductor. All three are vitally important, both for orchestras to properly play a symphony and for businesses to properly unify their people.

A Symphony

In Music: A large-scale musical composition, usually with four movements.

In Business: A shared language that impacts your organization, internally and externally, composed of four movements.

An Orchestra

In Music: A group of musicians with a variety of instruments, which can perform a symphony.

In Business: A team of people with a variety of skills, that can speak the *Shared Language of Success* and unify others.

A Conductor

In Music: A leader who understands the score and how it's supposed to sound. They give guidance and direction to create the desired result.

In Business: A leader who understands the purpose and how to impact people. They give guidance and direction to create the desired result.

When it comes to improving the language in your organization, and the impact it makes throughout, it is often the smallest adjustments that make the greatest impact. So, let's take a look at the fine-tuning required to enable our teams to communicate using the *Shared Language of Success.*

LANGUAGE ASSESSMENT

Communication Tuning

Gauge the tuning of your communication before attempting to unify. Rank each, on a scale of 1-10, 10 being best.

Our people speak our *business language*	1 2 3 4 5 6 7 8 9 10
Our *four movements* unify our team	1 2 3 4 5 6 7 8 9 10
Communication is a *two-way* experience	1 2 3 4 5 6 7 8 9 10
Our leaders *initiate* deeper dialogue	1 2 3 4 5 6 7 8 9 10
Communication is *intentionally* uplifting	1 2 3 4 5 6 7 8 9 10
Nonverbal signals are positive	1 2 3 4 5 6 7 8 9 10
Tone and *tact* are purposeful	1 2 3 4 5 6 7 8 9 10
Intent is always understood	1 2 3 4 5 6 7 8 9 10
We convey *optimism* during challenges	1 2 3 4 5 6 7 8 9 10
Our people have a *voice* (insights)	1 2 3 4 5 6 7 8 9 10
All forms of communication are *uplifting*	1 2 3 4 5 6 7 8 9 10
Communication training is *consistent*	1 2 3 4 5 6 7 8 9 10

PART I

The WORDS We Choose

You never know how long your words will stay in someone's mind, long after you spoke them.

~ Anonymous

Part I

The WORDS We Choose

Every Word Delivers a Meaning.

"Sticks and stones may break my bones but names will never hurt me." We were all taught to say this childhood rhyme to increase our resiliency against the devastating effects of name-calling – the *words* that cut through us like fiery daggers when we were young. Our parents said this to us as a way to keep us calm, avoid harmful retaliation, and ultimately to feel better. But we all know the truth and remember the painful sting of the words someone chose to hurt us; to tear us down; to make us feel inadequate.

Every word has a significant amount of power, either positive or negative. Our choice of words impacts how our communication is interpreted and creates a significant impact on us, both personally and professionally. In the workplace, especially, we must make a clear distinction of the type of words we choose. Failure to recognize the impact of our words may inadvertently cause an outcome we were not intending.

The National Centre Against Bullying, states that "While verbal bullying can start off harmless, it can escalate to levels which start affecting the individual target." Our choice of words can significantly impact others and according to Just Say YES, "Words are powerful. When it comes to bullying, sometimes verbal bullying can result in deeper wounds, long-term, than physical bullying."

While most people are not trying to bully people in the workplace, the impact of poorly chosen words can create an environment that tears apart the fibers of your culture. Left "untuned," the use of non-empowering words will build up walls that were never designed to be there. To say that words are powerful would be a huge understatement. Is your team harnessing the power of each word they choose to speak or are they haphazardly allowing the wrong words to create an unintentional emotional reaction?

Sound Bite:
Choose your words wisely – they define your character and impact your results.

The worst-case scenario is when a business has a person, or people, who intentionally chose words that undermine. When that person happens to be a leader, the impact is magnified.

UNDERSTANDING WORDS

According to Yehuda Berg, "Words are singularly the most powerful force available to humanity. We can choose to use this force constructively with words of encouragement, or destructively using words of despair. Words have energy and power with the ability to help, heal, hinder, hurt, harm, humiliate, and humble."

To speak properly, it goes without saying that we must use the correct words in our sentences. No one would argue with that, especially Mrs. Blank, my English teacher from 11th grade. Boy, she was a stickler for proper English and drove home her expertise to her students every day.

As we were taught in school, every word we speak falls into categories called word classes, based on the part they play in a sentence. Flashing back to our English classes we may remember the nine main word classes. It is important to understand the meaning of each word class.

The 9 Main Word Classes:

- A NOUN refers to a person, place, or thing.
- A VERB refers to an action, event, or state.

- A PRONOUN is a word that substitutes for noun phrases.
- An ADVERB modifies or qualifies an adjective.
- An ADJECTIVE describes people, animals, or things.
- A PREPOSITION expresses a relation to another word.
- A CONJUNCTION shows a link between words and phrases.
- A DETERMINER shows what type of reference the noun is making.
- An INTERJECTION is a word that shows a reaction.

We would all agree that the appropriate use of words in each class is essential for "proper speech." But I feel that we are missing a vitally important word class, one that is not taught in schools or businesses. So, I created the tenth class.

The 10th Word Class™:

- Magnet

This class provides the opportunity for engaging speech. To bring people together, it goes without saying that we must choose *magnetic* words.

- A MAGNET is a word that repels or unifies people.

Each day, people in the workplace use *Word Magnets* but most fail to realize or harness the inherent power their words have.

MAGNETIC COMMUNICATION

Without getting too deep into the science of magnets, there are two main types: permanent magnets and electromagnets. The permanent magnet is "always on," generating its own persistent magnetic field. An electromagnet requires an electric current to generate its magnetic field, which can be turned on and off with the flick of a switch.

The ends of a magnet are referred to as its poles. When magnets are lined up, so that two of the same poles face each other, they will push away. This is referred to as *repulsion*. When magnets are aligned, so that two opposite poles face each other, they will pull each other closer. This is called *attraction*. Ironically, magnetic attraction is 5-10% stronger than repulsion.

Magnets are part of our everyday existence and can be found inside of computers, in doorbells, in radios, in our cell phones, and are used in the medical field - MRI (*magnetic* resonance imaging). But perhaps the most important function is to post our children's artwork on the fridge.

Sound Bite:
Words are like magnets, with the power to attract people as well as repel them.

Magnets are also used every day in our communication but most people are unaware of their properties. *Word Magnets* give us the power to attract people to us or repel them away from us based on which ones we choose. Imagine our words creating a magnetic field that allows one or the other to occur – it's our choice. Before you speak, think about the magnetic effect you are intending.

The 2 Types of Word Magnets:

1. Attraction Words
2. Repulsion Words

Being aware of the words you choose will put you in control of the magnetic results you achieve. We all have the option of building those around us or tearing them down with our selection of words. Our words are powerful and they deliver meaning each time we speak. When we fail to understand the meaning behind each word, we leave room for misinterpretations and misunderstandings, both result in *Repulsion Words*.

WORDS ARE COSTLY

There are 171,476 words in the Second Edition of the Oxford English Dictionary, each with its own unique definitions and meanings. While most can be used in the workplace, there are a handful of obvious ones that should never be spoken, nor can I write them here. Words like *&@$, #@^&-*&^, and !@$# could be grounds for immediate termination.

Communication is the most powerful tool that we humans possess and the most critical element is our words! Together, we are going to examine the use of *Repulsion Words* that are too often used in the workplace and are like the off-key notes in a symphony. They have a costly impact on our cultures, our people, and our businesses.

It's time to introduce *Attraction Words* and *unify* our people. To do that, we are going to fine-tune our communication and focus on the three key benefits of choosing magnetic words, so they pull our people together.

Sound Bite:
Be aware of the communication "notes" you are playing. One off-key note can damage the entire symphony.

The Three Magnetic Benefits of our WORDS:

1. Build Strong Identities
2. Create Exceptional Attitudes
3. Assemble Remarkable Teams

Communication Catalyst

Magnetic Words

Description: This exercise identifies the *Magnetic Words* that should be used more frequently to unify people.

Time of Exercise: 60 minutes

Purpose: Team members discover and discuss the words that need to be spoken in your organization.

Resources: 3x5 cards, pens, white board, white board markers.

Presentation:

- Give a 3x5 card and a pen to each participant.
- Ask participants to list as many *Attraction Words* as possible in 5 minutes on their 3x5 cards. Examples include Enthusiasm, Teamwork, Empowerment, Collaboration.
- Go around and have each participant share their words as someone lists each word on a white board. Denote words mentioned more than once by putting the number of times each word occurred.
- Have an open discussion, choosing certain words and what they mean to each participant. Why did they list them? How can they increase using them and positively impact others?
- Create a final list of all words and add a shared definition to each one.

Debrief: Distribute your list of *Attraction Words* to everyone in your organization. Discuss them in meetings and one-on-ones. Continue to add to the list and encourage *Attraction Words* to be spoken fluently by your entire team.

Chapter 1

Build Strong Identities

The Tools that Strengthen Your Culture.

"I'd like to have a *word* with you."

"Put in a good *word* for me."

"What's the good *word*?"

Wow! One *word* can have so many meanings; so many interpretations. The first statement means that someone wants to talk. The next is asking for a favorable statement to be made. The last is asking about any good news.

When spoken in a spiritual context the *Word* expresses or manifests the mind and will of God. Before we speak, we must consider the meaning of the words we choose. Our failure to understand the meaning of our words does not eliminate peoples' interpretations of them.

The First Amendment of the Constitution of the United States:

"Congress shall make no law respecting an establishment of religion, or prohibiting the free exercise thereof; or abridging the freedom of speech, or of the press; or the right of the people peaceably to assemble, and to petition the Government for a redress of grievances."

The First Amendment protects five freedoms: speech, religion, press, assembly, and the right to petition the government. But it is often referred to as the amendment of *Free Speech*. Although speech may be free, there is a cost when it is delivered incorrectly in the workplace – when it repels our people instead of attracting them. Those little word magnets pack a punch.

Considering the unlimited power of the words we utter, we must focus on choosing words that convey our true meaning. Before speaking, we should always contemplate our words, our tone, and our intended message. Consider the impact that each word will have on those who hear it. In addition to choosing words that foster high levels of encouragement and inspiration, let's begin to select words that create cohesion. Unifying words are music to the ears of your team.

So, let's take a closer look at the definition of the word *word* and how we can magnetize our dialogue to *attract* our people.

word

noun

- a single distinct <u>meaningful</u> element of speech or writing, used with others (or sometimes alone) to form a sentence.
- a speech sound or series of speech sounds that <u>symbolizes</u> and communicates a meaning.
- a verbal <u>signal</u>.

Are the spoken words in your environment providing meaning? What do they symbolize? Are they verbal signals? I love that last definition. Yes, every word we choose is a verbal signal, sending powerful messages to everyone in earshot. What signals are being sent in your workplace? Are they warning signals or encouragement signals? Do they repel or do they attract?

NEGATIVE COMMUNICATION VS. POSITIVE COMMUNICATION

Coaching businesses has led me to a rather unique discovery – a phenomenon that exists in every organization. Negativity travels faster than positivity. When a leader or a team member says something that repels people, that message is interpreted and re-interpreted as it travels throughout your organization at the speed of light. Conversely, when a leader or team member says something positive, the flow of that message is typically slower.

Bad news hits immediately while good news may end up in the monthly newsletter. Now you know why people ask, "What's the good *word*?" We are inundated with the quickness of negativity but long for positivity. I have also found that while negativity may spread faster, positivity is stronger. We just don't focus our efforts on making it happen enough. Remember, magnetic attraction is 5-10% stronger than repulsion. Imagine all of the unlimited possibilities as negativity is replaced with positivity.

Sound Bite:
Negativity may travel faster than positivity but positivity is infinitely stronger.

Too many people in the workplace feel compelled to verbalize any thought that pops in their heads, unloading their words without regard to the negative impact of what they are saying. This may easily lead to gossip, negativity, complaining, and derogatory dialogue. Every organization has been severely impacted by these types of communication. Each type builds walls, places wedges between people, and affects morale.

Is there hope? Yes! When we decide to choose unifying words, we bring people together as we bring our identity to life.

JARGON CREATES IDENTITY

Every profession has its own unique jargon; doctors, lawyers, scientists, truck drivers, and fitness trainers use words that others may find odd. But they become part of their culture, allowing the members of that team to feel a part of their environments as they embrace this critical part of their identity. The right words bond people, like the attractive quality of magnets.

Jargon is defined as "special words or expressions that are used by a particular profession or group and are difficult for others to understand." In my experience, the workplace that uses jargon to its full capability – unifying their people, is the military. Not only does a shared language exist in the Armed Services, but it also thrives.

As an air traffic controller, I used specialized words like "Affirmative, Altitude, Caution, Roger, Runway, Taxi, Wilco. Each word had a specific meaning but these words fell into the category of our *Business* Language; the language required to perform our jobs.

The shared language of the Marines unified us in such a way that I still use some of those words when I meet another Marine, even though we never served together, and we both may have served decades apart. The right jargon spreads like wildfire, acting as a bonding tool – people want to speak it. It gives them a sense of belonging when they can talk to another member of their culture who shares their identity.

Jargon is not required to be understood by outsiders. It is strictly expressions of common experiences and challenges that allow us to understand each other. From the moment I stepped off the bus and began boot camp, our Drill Instructors delivered Marine Corps jargon. Here is a very small percentage of the words that I learned in the first few weeks of basic training.

Marine Corps JARGON (Words):

- **BELOW**   = Downstairs
- **BRIG**   = Military jail

- **BULKHEAD** = Wall
- **CAMMIES** = Camouflage uniform
- **COVER** = Hat
- **CHOW** = Food
- **DECK** = Floor
- **GEEDUNK** = Another term for food, usually a snack
- **HATCH** = Door/doorway
- **HEAD** = Bathroom/restroom
- **HUMP** = Field march
- **JARHEAD** = Name for a Marine (be careful using this one)
- **LEAVE** = Vacation time
- **LIBERTY** = Rest and relaxation/Authorized absence
- **KLICK** = A kilometer
- **LIFER** = Career Marine
- **PIECE** = Rifle
- **SCUTTLEBUTT** = Rumor; gossip/water fountain
- **SECURE** = Lock up, close, take care of, finish for the day
- **RACK** = Bed
- **SKIVVIES** = Underwear
- **TOPSIDE** = Upstairs
- **SWAB** = Mop
- **YUT** = An exclamation of excitement and camaraderie

It was a lot to learn and our DIs gave us zero time to acclimate to our new language. Despite the immeasurable challenges we faced, I found that our jargon, our words, provided us with a unification that was unlike anything I had ever felt. The bond was strong. We wanted to speak this language – it represented *who* we were, not just what we did.

Each branch of service has its own long list of words, acronyms, and colloquialisms that are unique to that branch, further strengthening the bond among fellow Soldiers, Sailors, Airmen, and Marines. Yet, there exist some common words. Each branch of service refers to a hat as a *cover.* And we all refer to the flag as *colors.*

Sound Bite:
Words are the building blocks of identity.

You do not need to incorporate military jargon in your culture, nor would it help to unify your people. I recommend that you diligently take a closer look at the words currently being used and the impact they are having. In many cases, *repulsion* words are being used so frequently that they have become commonplace.

It's time to replace some of the words being spoken by your people. Words are important but don't change anything in your current language! Wait a minute! I know what you're thinking – this is a book about *changing* our language, right? Absolutely not. This is a book about *enhancing* your language.

DON'T "CHANGE" ANYTHING!

Because every word sends a message, it is critically important to be aware of the meaning before we speak it. As a coach, I have observed the use of words, in every business, that are so commonly used, but with a simple replacement, they could generate an attractive impact. In the list of words to remove from your language, I am going to recommend the first word to replace is *Change.*

There's a popular saying that *change is constant.* That may be true but it does not alter the inherently negative perceptions that people have of this word. I know that some of you are already thinking, "I love change." But what I have found is that it is a common response to people trying to fight off the negative, repulsive impact that this word raises.

Change is different – enhancement is better.

Change causes some of the highest levels of resistance in an organization – the complete opposite of *attraction*.

Many organizations hire change agents to roll out a "change." Why? Because people already fear and hate change, some are even terrified of it. That's right, regardless of how positive the "change" is, it can create levels of terror.

Feelings about the word CHANGE:

- High levels of uncertainty
- Fear of the unknown
- Things are different
- Loss of control
- Creates more work
- Increases stress
- Lack of trust

Can one word have such an impact? Yes! The use of this word manifests itself in many ways, from foot-dragging and complacency to petty sabotage and outright rebellions. But we use them frequently, without thinking about

Sound Bite:
Change nothing – Enhance everything.

During my time as the vice president of the media company, I knew that a significant amount of change would be required to accomplish our business of doubling our annual sales revenue. I also knew that the perceptions of change would slow us down, so I began to describe all the enhancements we would make. Instead of jeers, I heard cheers.

The same anxiety caused by *changing* our sales system was now replaced with the excitement of *enhancing* our sales system. People have different perceptions of this word and their enthusiasm and performance led me to focus on enhancing things, not changing things.

Feelings about the word ENHANCE:

- Advancement made
- Increasing
- Strengthening
- Innovation
- Enlightenment

This is why most strategic plans fail to gain elevation. Everything in a plan is perceived as a change – different. Your strategic plan (what we at Think GREAT call a Flight Plan) should only include enhancements, so you can receive the buy-in from those striving to be better – greater!

Replacing *change* with *enhance* made a significant impact. Just one word shifted paradigms, enhanced perceptions, impacted performance, and increased buy-in. Then I had an idea. With our business filled with leaders and teams, perhaps there were additional words that would help with our dreams. Maybe words, I thought, shouldn't be spoken by chance, maybe words, perhaps, allow us to advance. Ok, I'm a huge fan of Dr. Seuss. His timeless use of words still impacts children (and many adults) around the world today. Imagine the possibilities as you begin to replace words of repulsion with words of attraction in your business.

NEVER "MANAGE" PEOPLE!

When I ask business leaders and team members, "What is the greatest asset in your company?" I always receive the same unanimous reply - "People." Regardless of what industry we work in, leadership is the people aspect of our business. Unfortunately, many people who hold leadership positions are not developed as leaders, and they are often intertwining the words leadership and management much to their detriment.

Using Google for a moment, let's look up both words. Leadership revealed 2.5 billion results and management ended with 7.3 billion results. Both words are not only defined differently but also have different meanings to people. Unfortunately, leaders unintentionally misuse the words, causing unnecessary levels of repulsion.

As soon as I hear, "I'm having trouble managing my people," I know where a huge part of the problem lies. When I conduct leadership workshops, filled with hundreds of people, I always ask, "Is there a difference between leading and managing?" The speed with which everyone answers a resounding "Yes" is staggering. Interestingly, when I ask what the difference is, many struggle to articulate it.

That struggle is a huge factor in the identity of your entire organization and a catalyst for disengagement. I have a simple philosophy, manage the work – lead your people. We should manage budgets, projects, shift schedules, and inventory. Never manage people. We need to lead our people – guide them, mentor them, coach them, encourage them, and engage them. When people feel like they are being managed, it is easy for them to feel micro-managed, macro-managed, or poorly managed.

Sound Bite:
Manage the work – Lead your people.

As a coach, people often express to me their reasons for leaving a company. Guess what the number one reason is? You guessed it, "Poor management." I have never had anyone tell me they are leaving because of strong leadership. Leadership is the foundation upon which we build everything. You cannot afford to reduce its impact on management

For the record, I work with hundreds of "managers," people who have management titles. Their difference – they made the decision to fulfill their leadership purpose, not just fill a leadership position. I have been a manager many times over. I was a vault manager, operations manager, and branch office manager. Regardless of my title, I was wrapped in leadership. I managed the work and led my people.

We will dive more into the leadership words needed to create movement but you can also check out my book *The LEADERSHIP Connection* to learn how to guide your people on a *Leadership Expedition*.

STOP "SELLING"

I'll bet I have your attention now. Did he just say, "Stop Selling?" You bet I did. I hate selling even though I know it's the lifeblood of every organization. I even wrote a sales book, and I'll repeat the theme throughout that entire book. Stop selling!

When I train sales professionals, I ask them to tell me the words that come to mind when I say, *salesperson*. They often say things like pushy, shady, money-hungry, and aggressive, to name a few. Ironically, those are the first words that came to their minds and they are the ones selling. Imagine the words that come to mind from the buyers.

The perceptions of that one word, *selling*, conjures up a myriad of emotions. Mostly negative, and typically how we have been burned in the past by someone in sales. Stop selling!

No salesperson likes selling as much as they like "getting a sale." Most salespeople find things to keep them *busy* (yes, we will discuss that word, too) and tend to avoid selling because of the negativity attached to that word. Unfortunately, antiquated sales training still exists and encourages people to get out there and *sell*.

As Think GREAT grew (people were buying), I knew that I would need someone to increase our outreach. I needed to hire a Director (not manager) of Business Development (not sales), for Think GREAT. I was excited about all of the energy and passion that one particular person could bring to the table.

When I told Sandy about the opportunity, she was excited, but that feeling quickly faded as she regretfully said, "But I can't sell." That was music to my ears and I replied with. "Great! Because, if you sold anything, I'd have to fire you." She stared at me for a moment and

I said, "I don't want you to sell anything to anyone. Can you *share* the impact we make on people?" Her reply was not only priceless (literally), but it was the feeling we needed.

"I could do that all day long," she said confidently. She has been doing that all day long for over five years! How would you like for your salespeople to eagerly hop on the phone and excitedly set face-to-face appointments? How would you like them to ooze passion and belief, while simultaneously building your organization's reputation... and increasing the action of "buying?"

 **Sound Bite:**
People are more likely to buy when you stop selling your products and begin sharing your solutions.

I love it when my clients let me know that they are having history-making months in sales. It is not a fluke that it tends to happen as their people stop *selling* and start *sharing*. According to the dictionary, one definition of *share* is to tell (thoughts, feelings, experiences, etc.) to others. Because buying is an emotional experience for most buyers, it makes sense that your people are sharing their thoughts, feelings, and experiences to guide people on their emotional journey to buy.

Sandy has never sold anything. But she has opened the door to so much buying. As we dive more into the sales words you need to create a movement, you can also check out my book *Dynamic Sales COMBUSTION* to learn how to win championships on the *Sales Speedway* with your team.

CHANCE VS. CHOICE

"Over and out." We've all heard these words on television shows, in the movies, and by military wannabees. As a kid growing up, I even said this when playing cops and robbers with my friends. But as I learned in the military, both words have significantly different meanings when properly communicating with a two-way radio.

- Over – I am finished talking and <u>await a reply</u>.
- Out   – I am finished talking and <u>do not need a reply</u>.

In essence, over and out means "I am finished talking and do not need a reply but I am waiting for a reply." Combining these words creates a contradiction. Our choice of words is paramount. But most people fail to think before they speak in the workplace. When we unintentionally choose our words, we intentionally unleash all their power; the perceptions, feelings, and emotions they carry with them. Of course, that power could be negative or positive. There is far too much at stake to risk it.

Not only do our words matter, but they set the tone for our entire culture. They are building blocks of our identity and we must use them, not only to communicate but to connect our people.

The choice is yours. Do as I have done and replace the words that push people away with the words that pull them together. I no longer *change* anything; I *enhance* everything. I refuse to *manage* people; I love to *lead* people. I never *sell*; I always *share*. I make the choice to use *magnetic* words.

REPULSION	ATTRACTION
• Change	• Enhance
• Manage (people)	• Lead (people)
• Sell	• Share

Enhance, *Lead*, and *Share* are powerful words, with attractive qualities that will begin to unify your people. Those *Word Magnets* have allowed my teams to experience exponential growth and they will do the same for your team. But they are only three of the 171,476 words we have access to.

Communication Catalyst

Replacing Our Words

Description: This exercise identifies words that may be causing repulsion (pushing people away), and what their replacement words will be.

Time of Exercise: 60 minutes

Purpose: Team members acknowledge the words being used in your workplace that need to be "enhanced" and identify the new words to replace them.

Resources: 3x5 cards, pens, white board, white board markers.

Presentation:

- Give a 3x5 card and a pen to each participant.
- Ask participants to identify any words of repulsion that need to be replaced. Examples include Employee vs. Team Member, Managing vs. Leading, and Change vs. Enhance.
- On one side of the white board, list the "Repulsion" words.
- Next, have team members offer suggestions of the words to replace and list them on the right-hand side under "Attraction."
- Create a final list of all the words being eliminated and their replacements.

Debrief: Share your list of Repulsion Words and the Attraction Words to replace them. Discuss the importance of using these replacement words in specific scenarios.

Chapter 2

Create Exceptional Attitudes

Paint a Picture of Enthusiasm.

Serving in the military, I realized quickly that everything had meaning and purpose, including our words like *deck*, our phrases like *Ooh-Rah*, our gestures like *a hand salute*, and our actions like *gas chamber qualification*. Nothing was done "just because." With lives at stake, there was a high value placed on relevancy, in everything we did – and everything we said.

I had been indoctrinated in a culture that understood the power of words and used them masterfully to unify their people. Each word had a meaning that was understood by each Marine, Sailor, Soldier, and Airman. This was part of our focus on cohesion and our unwavering bond with fellow service members. Unfortunately, after my tour of duty ended in 1991, I noticed that the same focus on word choice did not exist in the business sector.

A few weeks after completing my tour of duty in the Marine Corps, I began my studies at Orange Coast College, in Costa Mesa, California. While I was attending class, I worked different jobs to put myself through school and support my family. I worked at a small video rental store, at a grocery store, and at K-Mart. While each company spoke their *Business Language* – the important words to run their organization – they failed to unify people based on their choice of magnetic words.

Choosing the right words would have formed positive, can-do attitudes while encouraging high levels of initiative. Instead, they opted for words that had the opposite effect. But why would anyone intentionally use words that push their people away? For starters, they were not vulgar or even offensive words. The words we are about to analyze are commonly used in most workplace environments. But they have unfortunate side effects; side effects that produce long-lasting damage.

WHAT PICTURE ARE YOU PAINTING?

When we fail to understand the impact of the words consistently spoken in our environments, we may inadvertently select words that negatively impact our people, causing hidden layers of resentment, disengagement, and frustration. In turn, these words affect our teams' morale, performance, and results. When we use these poorly chosen words in our workplace, it's like painting the inside of our homes with the wrong paint.

No, I'm not referring to your color choice. I'm describing words that are more like lead-based paint, which was commonly used in homes built prior to 1960. Medical and scientific research shows that the absorption of even the smallest levels of lead into the bloodstream may have devastating health effects on the intellectual and behavioral development of infants and young children.

According to HealthLinkBC, "Since 2010, paint in Canada containing more than 0.009% lead must be labeled to indicate that it is not safe to use in areas accessible to children or pregnant women." After seeing the evidence and data, it seems crazy to use lead paint today. But it was done for decades because the harm could not be immediately seen. In 1992, all consumer paints produced in Canada and America were replaced with lead-free versions.

Certain words are like drops of lead paint, slowly contaminating our environments, each time they are spoken. Just like lead-based paint, the true damage of these words cannot be immediately seen or felt. Like buckets of lead paint, we must replace the repulsive words spilling out of our people, so we can paint a better picture in the workplace – an environment of unification, cohesion, and teamwork.

Sound Bite:
Every word spoken is like a drop of paint – slowly covering our culture and our people.

By the time I began working at the media company, I had been immersed in the business sector for twelve years and had become accustomed to consistently hearing people use these words. Because they had not been taught the power and meaning of their words, they unintentionally painted a picture that resulted in low morale and lackluster results. In 2003, I took an entry-level position at the media company, and again, those little words were spoken fluently and painted a picture that did not match our desired vision.

The owner of the company wanted to double sales and I knew that we were only going to get there if our people had *exceptional attitudes.* There was a tremendous opportunity in front of us and I wanted to do more than accomplish his goal, I wanted to surpass it. I analyzed the language in our culture and quickly realized that it did not support our goals. We had good people but we were not unified. We had experienced people but we were not cohesive. Our language did little to create exceptional attitudes.

Just like buckets of old lead paint, we had certain words that needed to be discarded and replaced, especially if we were serious about hitting our lofty objectives. I began to make some suggestions on words we should stop uttering and the words we should start speaking. By now, I know you must be thinking, "What are the words he is talking about?"

In addition to replacing words like, *change, manage,* and *sell,* I have discovered another set of words that impact the overall attitudes of our people. These five words have significant power. Unfortunately, it's the power of slowly pushing people away – contaminating their mindsets. The replacements that I will recommend have the effect of pulling people together and creating exceptional attitudes - for the person speaking them and the people hearing them.

GET RID OF YOUR "EMPLOYEES"

"Whoa, what did he say?" Did he really recommend getting rid of everyone? No, of course not. But I did make a simple suggestion that aligned with the vision of our media company. I have found that most business leaders say one thing but use words that describe something completely different, causing subtle hints of confusion. The owner often referred to everyone as being part of a team, which is a good thing, right?

It absolutely is but our word choices did not help to build a *team.* When I served in the Marines, I received a paycheck. I was employed by the United States Marine Corps but I was never referred to as an *employee.* I was a Marine, a Jarhead, a Devil Dog, a Leatherneck. We were never reduced to being an employee. The Marines referred to us as a team and their descriptions of their people supported that claim. Many business leaders refer to their people as a team but their words often contradict that claim.

Think about the impact of referring to people as mere employees. Although it is said a billion times per day, remember that every word has power. This is a word that does absolutely nothing to unify your *team.* Can *employee* be that bad? Yes! Think about all of the people you work with. When they were in high school, and their counselors asked, "What do you want to be when you grow up?" Do you think a single one of them answered, "I want to be an employee"? Of course not.

Can you imagine going home and telling your parents, "I decided to be an employee." I know my dad would have pulled me aside and said, "Son, I need to have a *word* with you." But again, this is just one of many words that paint the picture of mediocrity and unintentionally amplify disengagement. After all, let's look at the difference in the definitions of *employee* and *team member.*

Employee: a person employed for wages or salary, especially at a non-executive level.

Team Member: A person belonging to a collection of people involved in achieving a common goal.

Do you want people in your business who are merely looking for a paycheck or those who are looking for a purpose? To double sales at the media company, we needed people focused on common goals. We needed a cohesive team and we could not afford to only deliver lip service. I remember asking the owner if he would be open to *enhancing* (not *changing*) our Employee Handbook. He said, "Yeah, what do you have in mind?"

I expressed the need for a team to accomplish our goals and mentioned that we indirectly refer to our people as our *employees*, even in our handbook, which repeated the word over one hundred times. "What if we started referring to them as team members?" I asked. He embraced the word shift and I notified our HR consultant to remove every mention of *employee* from our handbook and replace it with *team member.* When we received the updated version of our Team Member Handbook, we re-issued it to everyone during a "team" meeting.

We expressed our belief in the *team* and also re-announced our goals. Could one word make an impact? Yes, and it did. We let the team know that they were not *employees* to us. Everyone was a valuable member of our team and we began to express it to them constantly.

Sound Bite:
To experience the true power of a team, hire and build team members, not employees.

The choices we make with our words set the parameters for our work environments and contribute to the overall attitudes of our people. The real power in words stems from the meaning, interpretation, and feelings experienced by the people hearing them.

TEAM VS. GROUP

Now that we have replaced employees with team members, we need to ensure that we actually have a real team. When I ask business leaders to tell me about their people, they refer to them as an elite team, with the best of intentions. But when I ask them to describe the collective efforts and results of their people, they most often describe the actions of an average group.

I love going to concerts. The energy, the screaming fans, and the music – pure excitement. I enjoy the complete experience of watching and listening to my favorite music *groups* performing on stage. But I also enjoy the experience of going to sporting events. When I watch sports, there is also a lot of energy and screaming fans. But the music is replaced with competition as I watch my favorite sports *teams*.

When I want to experience winning, I need the power of a team, not a group. If you want to unify your people and experience more winning, you need to have a team, not a group. There is a huge difference between both in the workplace. You want team members, not group members because you need teamwork, not "groupwork," right? If you said yes, then we need to look at the difference in the definitions of a *group* and *team*.

Group: a number of people that are located close together or are considered or classed together.

Team: a number of persons associated together in work or activity; to achieve a common goal.

There is nothing wrong with people in a group, but their proximity to one another hardly classifies them as a team. It does not mean that they are doing bad things but it also may indicate that they are not doing *team* things. You need to ask yourself a question, do you want a *group* of *employees* or a *team* of people who think and act as *leaders*? The choice is yours, so select your *magnetic* words carefully.

Sound Bite:
If you want to harness the power of a team, you need teamwork, not groupwork.

Too many leaders use the words *group* and *team* interchangeably. They are absolutely different and bring about different perceptions, performance, and results. A *group* is a gathering of individuals who perform their individual efforts. A *team*, however, is a collection of team members who coordinate their actions to accomplish common objectives and achieve shared results. Which would you prefer to have working on your goals?

When we choose magnetic words to attract people, we can use them in the interview process, too. When I interviewed future *team members*, I asked each candidate, "How do you feel about being part of a team, part of a cohesive unit that's focused on common goals?"

These were powerful words that I used in the interview to paint the picture of our culture and what they could expect if we chose them. Because I chose Words of Attraction to set the tone, it was not uncommon, after an interview, for people to say things like, "I would love to be part of your team," or "I'll do whatever it takes to join this team."

STOP BEING "BUSY"

I hear *busy* in the workplace more than I hear teenagers say *like*. Like, you know, it is one of the greatest Words of Repulsion but everyone is speaking it. "How was your day?" "Oh, I was so busy." Perhaps you've asked someone for help and they replied, "I would love to help but I'm too busy."

When someone says, "I'm so busy," it is often interpreted as "my work is more important than yours." Again, every word has a meaning and *busy* is often perceived as an excuse rather than a reason. When I ask people if there is a difference between being busy and being productive, I always receive a resounding "Yes!"

When I ask people to describe "busy" work, they use words such as meaningless, mundane, and non-important. So, when someone says, "I'm too busy to help with that project, objective, or goal," they are essentially saying. "I would like to help with that essential action but I am doing mundane, meaningless, non-important work." No one has ever told me; I'd like to help but I'm too *productive*.

Sound Bite:
Eliminate all busy work and replace it with productive work.

To me, *busy* is a code word for "I'm not fully engaged" or "I do not fully trust you." Busy work is perceived as having little to no value, whereas productivity is perceived as meaningful, important, and critical. Productive teams operate with the unwritten motto of "let's do more with less." Busy work also has its own motto – "let's do less with more." Once again, our words help to dictate the attitudes in our environment.

Let's take a close look at the difference between *busy work* and *productive work.*

Busy Work: work that keeps a person busy but has little value in itself; to pass time.

Productive Work: The effectiveness of effort from a person, based on output and results.

When the boss is away, it's not uncommon for productivity to dip (not busyness). In some workplace environments, when the boss returns, *employees* will warn others that "the boss is coming... look *busy." Productive team members* do not operate like that, especially when they feel like they are part of a *team.* I never want a team of busy beavers or busy little bees.

Instead of being "busy," be "productive" or "have a packed schedule."

STOP "CLOSING" OPPORTUNITIES

"I just closed them!" I remember hearing salespeople return to the office and proudly announce that after a field appointment. I should have been excited to see someone return with a sale but something always sounded slightly wrong to me knowing that someone had just been closed. Could they possibly have had an appointment with a family member or a friend? Would they close one of their family members or a dear friend?

When sales professionals focus on *closing* people or *closing* sales, their mindset has now limited their ability for achieving higher performance. Although most would view a *closed* sale as a step toward earning more money, I believe they unintentionally *closed* new opportunities to accomplish their goals faster.

I often notice that when colleagues asked how the appointment went, I heard the sales professional discussing how they *closed* the person or *closed* the sale. They described what was purchased, but not how the client had benefitted. I'm sure they did help their clients but their dialogue did not reflect it. In fact, the bigger the sale that was *closed*, the more high-fives the salesperson received.

Making money is not a bad thing but the words we focus on shape our attitudes, which dictate our destiny. Like most sales professionals, I attended sales trainings to help me to develop the skills to be more successful. Unfortunately, the antiquated training always seemed to revolve more around *selling* and *closing*, not *sharing* and *opening*.

Sound Bite:
Our words shape our attitudes and our attitudes dictate our destiny.

Instead of closing people or closing a sale, try opening... open new dialogue; open the relationship; open new opportunities. Let's take a look at the meaning of both words.

Close: to block against entry or passage.

Open: having no enclosing or confining barrier.

Most salespeople say one thing to their clients and prospects but speak another language when they return to their offices. Could you imagine starting your appointment off with, "I'm really hoping to *close* you today?" The hypocrisy in sales exists in so many companies. When we focus on closing, our outcome is commission. When we focus on *opening*, our outcome is opportunities.

Regardless of the word you choose to use, you will give off an aura that is felt by everyone. Are you a closed sales professional or an open sales professional? If your buyer feels closed, will they be open to sending you referrals?

NEVER SET "QUOTAS"

While we're speaking about sales, I have had the opportunity to work with many sales teams. Along with the "old" way of training, there exists the old way of measuring performance – *quotas*. There is a need for sales professionals and sales teams to meet their *quotas* but this word is, unfortunately, often misused and overused in the sales world.

In its most basic form, a sales quota is used to determine the amount of revenue that a business needs to earn for the year. It can then be divided and set up as quarterly or monthly quotas, with salespeople being assigned a portion of the quota to hit. In its most basic form, a sales goal typically represents objectives to help a company grow, such as new markets, new products, or new key accounts. By this point in the book, you already know that everyone has their own definition of these two words – quotas and goals.

According to an article by MarketingProfs.com, "One sobering fact is that two-thirds of all salespeople miss their quotas. According to the research, 67% of sales professionals don't meet their individual quotas. Worst of all, 23% of companies don't even know whether their sales teams have achieved their quotas."

Quota assignments also lead to one of the major reasons that salespeople leave an organization. Again, we are looking at a word that has the magnetic effect of repulsion – pushing people away. So, let's take a look at the definition of both.

Quota: a fixed share of something that a person or group is bound to contribute.

Goal: the achievement toward which effort is directed.

Let's just get it out of the way immediately, salespeople hate quotas. Not because they are lazy or unmotivated but because the word quota is cold and forced, void of passion and enthusiasm. Quotas are another word with good intentions and poor results.

Sound Bite:
Quotas do little to motivate your salespeople. Sales goals provide purpose, hope, and focus.

When I started at the media company, there were already sales quotas in place. None of which were being hit or discussed. None of which provided a driving force to hit our sales goals, which, of course, had not been clearly established.

Removing our *quotas* was like unfastening the rope tying our boat to the dock. As we set sales goals, we began to set sail toward the achievement of each goal. We set individual sales goals for each sales professional. These sales goals aligned with their personal goals. We set sales goals for the sales team and we set sales goals for the entire company.

All of these goals were divided into 90-day goals, quarterly goals, annual goals, and 3-5-year goals. Sales quotas caused our *efforts* to be *fixed* but our sales *goals* allowed us to *move* toward our vision.

ZERO TOLERANCE

As a way to combat undesirable behavior in the workplace, many businesses establish zero-tolerance policies with the understanding that a violation equals termination. Examples include firearms, drugs, theft, harassment, and offensive words. Zero tolerance is implemented to protect our people and our businesses. I'm not going to argue the merits or results of these policies but rather to suggest a zero-tolerance approach to Words of Repulsion.

No, I'm not suggesting that you fire people for using these words but I am recommending that you teach them the words to be used as their replacements if you want to protect your people and your business from the negative magnetic effects of these words.

REPULSION	ATTRACTION
• Employee	• Team Member
• Group	• Team
• Busy	• Productive
• Closing	• Opening
• Quotas	• Goals

Every word is open to interpretation and comes with perceptions already attached to it. Because words can easily be incorrectly interpreted, be careful in the words you choose. They impact attitudes. I have found that many people spend more time choosing the right software for their business than the right words for their culture.

Communication Catalyst

Alphabet of Positivity

Description: At least 5 team members will select positive words to describe attributes of their colleagues.

Time of Exercise: 15 minutes

Purpose: To encourage team members to develop the habit of communicating positive messages as they use uplifting words to describe them.

Resources: Blank strips of paper, pens, small bowl.

Presentation:

- Give each team member a blank strip of paper and a pen, and have them write their name on it.
- Place names into a bowl.
- Everyone picks a name from the bowl. If they select their own name, they draw again.
- Starting with the letter A, everyone shares a positive word that begins with that letter to describe the person they selected.

Debrief: This is a great way to begin a meeting. There is no need to go through the entire alphabet in one sitting. This exercise can be highly effective by using 2-3 letters at a time, then continued with another 2-3 letters at the next meeting.

Encourage each department/team to utilize this exercise regularly.

Chapter 3

Assemble Remarkable Teams

Key Words that Transform People.

Could you imagine everyone speaking the same language, not just in the workplace, but throughout our entire world? Is it possible to unify over seven billion people with one dialect? In 1887, Polish ophthalmologist, Dr. Ludwik Lejzer Zamenhof attempted to do just that, creating an artificial language called Esperanto. Believing that all the current languages spoken divided people, he hoped to unify everyone and bring about world peace. He understood the power of words.

Although his creation did not deliver the intended outcome, his focus was not without merit. The importance of language for human beings and our cultures cannot be minimized. The words we speak are essential to every aspect and interaction in our lives. The words we speak in the workplace should be viewed as essential, too. Communication issues can negatively impact morale and productivity. Most importantly, it can undermine our attempts to unify our people and assemble remarkable teams.

Never heard of Esperanto? Most people have not, although there are currently 99 million results on Google for this language, including online courses to learn it. According to Ethnologue, there are approximately two million Esperantists who can speak it in some form. Some are so committed to the language that they have raised their children as native Esperanto speakers.

There are Esperanto meetups and conferences all around the world, and there are also Esperanto magazines and an Esperanto science journal. So why do Esperantists continue to speak a language that will never become universal? It all comes back to unification - language is identity and a strong identity leads to the creation of teams that can accomplish remarkable things.

According to the Linguistic Society of America, "As far back as we have written records of human language – 5,000 years or so," language has gradually evolved. However, the problem with constructed languages, like Klingon, Elvish, and even Esperanto, is that they are not native languages, so they do not evolve in the same way. Dr. Zamenhof had the vision but lacked the natural evolution necessary to strengthen the meaning of each word, allowing for the unification he had dreamed of.

BECOME AN ARTIST

When you serve in the military, you are immediately issued a ton of gear, everything from uniforms and toothbrushes to your rifle and gas mask. We carried our canteens, ammunition, sleeping bags, ponchos, shovels, and first aid kits. While the list goes on and on, one item always seemed out of place. Yet, it is provided to all members of each branch of service.

To assemble remarkable teams, those that operate in absolute cohesion, a special tool is required. The military paintbrush is perhaps the most critical piece of gear that is not issued – it is earned. You didn't know that the military issues paintbrushes with your taxpayer dollars, did you? While we never received a physical version of this vital tool, it is used each day to assemble the platoons, companies, and battalions of young men and women who guard our freedoms.

Leadership is undeniably the foundation of the military and when something is of the highest importance, you never leave it to chance. You select a magnetic *keyword* to describe it with exact precision so there are no misunderstandings and misinterpretations. Below are the definitions of leadership, from the handbooks available to every Airman, Soldier, Sailor, and Marine. They all chose the same *keyword* to set the tone for the caliber of their teams.

Air Force: "The _**art**_ of influencing and directing people in a way that will win their obedience, confidence, respect, and loyal cooperation in achieving a common objective or goal."

Army: "Leadership is paramount to our profession. It is integral to our institutional success today and tomorrow. You will face difficult decisions and dilemmas. This is all part of the process of learning the _**art**_ of leadership."

Navy: "Simply stated, leadership is the _**art**_ of accomplishing the Navy's mission through people. To accomplish this, the Navy leader employs the principles of leadership, core values, and the qualities that lead to success."

Marine Corps: "Leadership has passed from Marine to Marine since the founding of the Corps (1775). It is the _**art**_ of influencing and directing men and women to accomplish the mission of keeping our country free."

While each branch of the military is unique and differs in its tactics, they are unified on one magnetic _keyword_ to describe leadership, and a paintbrush is required to apply it.

Sound Bite:
When a concept is important in your business, choose a _keyword_ to express its deeper meaning.

When most people think about the military, I'm sure that images of camouflage uniforms, firefights, explosions, and hand-to-hand combat come to mind. I doubt they envisioned service members as artists. But even in the intense, life-and-death atmosphere of the military, art transforms the concept of leadership into something beautiful, creative, and artistic, not forced, abrupt, or controlling.

Leaders in the military work on their people like artists who work on canvas. _**Art**_ is their chosen _keyword_ for leadership, and that one single word has the power to enhance the perceptions of those who hear it.

When a powerfully magnetic word of attraction is spoken enough, it unifies the people who repeatedly hear it.

Most business leaders readily acknowledge the critical importance of leadership, just as their military counterparts do. Unfortunately, they struggle to define it. Service members do not have that problem because of the focus of their *keyword – art*. What keywords are you using to define important concepts and build remarkable teams?

CORE WORDS

What would you do if you found a treasure map that listed the exact spot of untold riches and fortunes? Would you take the steps to recover the gold and jewels or completely ignore it? "X" may mark the spot but when we fail to take the steps to get there, we are unable to reap the rewards in store for us.

In every business, there should exist *Core Words* that guide the way to untold levels of engagement and empowerment in our people. But like a treasure map that has been tossed aside, most businesses rarely uncover the true treasures buried within their people. You will unlock something greater than gold and jewels when you speak your *core values* - you unleash words with the power to unify your people and assemble remarkable teams.

With so much magnetic power, you can imagine that business leaders are speaking these words, often and with the highest levels of enthusiasm each day in their organizations, right? The unfortunate reality that I have discovered is that most core values get very little airtime. They are rarely spoken in the workplace, and worse yet, most people do not even know what they are. In some cases, business leaders have decided to not have any core values. The untapped power of *core values* lies in their own definitions.

Core: an essential part or meaning.

Value: something, such as a principle or quality, intrinsically valuable or desirable.

Individually, each word is powerful but the combined force of linking them together will magnetize your entire team, unifying everyone within reach. But in most businesses, core values are merely a checkbox item completed as part of some exercise that was long forgotten, just like a long-lost treasure map that was disregarded before the treasure was discovered.

By definition, core values are "essential principles and qualities of meaning and value" that should be identified and spoken, not solely posted on a wall or a website. Every business leader wants a remarkable team but most often do little to assemble them, based on their use of their *Core Words*; the words valued most in their business. I have found that many leaders are unable to recite their core values, while others struggle to identify the exact number they have. It's not a surprise that most team members have almost no recall of the core values of their company.

Far too many leaders fail to unify their teams and rarely utilize the highly magnetized Words of Attraction that represent their company's unwavering commitment – their core values. What is the perceived meaning of those words when they are never spoken? Can they truly be *core* or *valued*?

Sound Bite:
Core values that are not spoken hold no value.

Are your core values an option or an obligation? When they are spoken with confidence and consistency, they attract people, which is exactly what you need – people attracted to your core values. If those words repel some people, then that is a clear indicator that they should probably not be on your team.

From the time I entered my recruiter's office until the end of my tour of duty, four years later, three words unified the entire Marine

Corps - Honor, Courage, and Commitment. Their three core values are not mere suggestions; they are magnetic words that every member knows, understands, and is expected to exemplify. In addition to identifying their *Core Words*, they defined each word, so its meaning was crystal clear.

These three words are spoken, often and with great passion, so the power is not just heard, it is experienced. Here are the three core values of the Marine Corps and how they define each one.

HONOR

This is the bedrock of our character. It is the quality that empowers Marines to exemplify the ultimate in ethical and moral behavior: to never lie, cheat, or steal; to abide by an uncompromising code of integrity; to respect human dignity; to have respect and concern for each other. It represents the maturity, dedication, trust, and dependability that commit Marines to act responsibly, be accountable for their actions, fulfill their obligations, and hold others accountable for their actions.

COURAGE

The heart of our Core Values, courage is the mental, moral, and physical strength ingrained in Marines that sees them through the challenges of combat and the mastery of fear, and to do what is right, to adhere to a higher standard of personal conduct, to lead by example, and to make tough decisions under stress and pressure. It is the inner strength that enables a Marine to take that extra step.

COMMITMENT

This is the spirit of determination and dedication within members of a force of arms that leads to professionalism and mastery of the art of war. It promotes the highest order of discipline for unit and self and is the ingredient that instills dedication to Corps and country 24 hours a day, pride, concern for others, and an unrelenting determination to achieve a standard of excellence in every endeavor. Commitment is the value that establishes the Marine as the warrior and citizen others strive to emulate.

MAGNETIZE YOUR CORE VALUES

The power of those three *Core Words* has been instrumental in unifying Marines for generations. How often are your core values discussed and taught? Are they part of your onboarding for new team members? Are they part of your criteria for promotions? Does every member of your team know them? Does your business actually have core values and use them to assemble remarkable teams?

Regardless if you have core values or need to create them, their power, when used properly, is undeniable and will magnetize your people and allow you to harness their true potential. There are four ways to fully magnetize your core values and unify your people.

Four Ways to Magnetize Your Core Values:

1. Identify Your Core Values
2. Define Your Core Values
3. Teach Your Core Values
4. Share Your Core Values

Identify Your Core Values

If you already have Core Values, you are a step ahead. If not, invest the time to create the words that represent your *essential principles and qualities of meaning and value*. More than just trying to discover some popular or cool words, this is an incredibly unique opportunity to further unify your people.

Dedicate time with your leaders, and enlist the insights of your entire team, to identify your core values. Once you have a list of possible words that best represent your unwavering values, narrow the selection down to the three to five choices that, when spoken, magnetize your people.

Just because a word does not make the cut, does not mean it is not important. You may have additional values, guiding principles, or essential traits, but your core values are your *keywords* for unifying each member of your team. If you already have your core values, this is a great time to reassess their relevancy and decide if it is time to enhance them.

Define Your Core Values

Congratulations on choosing each of your core values. I know that a lot of thought went into their selection and you deserve to reap the benefits of those magnetic words. During the selection phase, you and your people were probably already thinking about the meaning of each word, and as we already know, every word has many meanings. So, this is an important step to develop one unifying definition of what each core value means to your organization.

Just as the Marine Corps defined *Honor, Courage*, and *Commitment*, you and your team must establish a deeper understanding of each word, to ensure that the expectations on personal and professional performance are in alignment with your *Core Words*. By definition, to *define* something is "to show or describe something clearly and completely." This is an exciting time to have in-depth discussions about your core values and what they mean – clearly and completely. Leave no room for misunderstandings.

Teach Your Core Values

Core values all suffer from one major weakness – ending up as mere words on a website or a wall. Once your values are crafted and each definition is set, it's time to breathe life into them. Teach your core values – internally to your team. Because your core values represent what your business stands for, start with the people standing for them. Core values should echo through the hallways of our buildings and be read in our e-mails sent.

Starting with your onboarding program, new members of your team should be indoctrinated with your core values and their definitions.

Your trainers should reference your core values while working with your people, and your leaders should exemplify them each day. They should be discussed in meetings and used as opportunities to course-correct behaviors and provide guidance to realign your team's performance with the expectations of your core values.

Sound Bite:
Used consistently, core values will transform your people and help to assemble a remarkable team.

Share Your Core Values

In addition to being taught consistently, core values should be shared on your website for all to experience and posted throughout your office for visitors to see. Share your core values – externally to those outside of your team. Let everyone know what you stand for, not just what you do. Your team should share them during the interview process with new candidates to establish the high-level expectations you have for their performance.

Share with your vendors to establish relationships that are deeper than your next order. Share with your existing clients and with your prospects. Instead of just asking for another sale, share your core values – why they should buy from you. At Think GREAT, one of our favorite follow-up touches is a one-page sheet about our identity. It details our Mission Statement and our Vision Statement. It also showcases our core values – Passion, Integrity, and Excellence (PIE). That is what we promise to deliver!

I know what you might be thinking. "Can core values be that important?" Give a U.S. Marine a mission, a task, or an assignment, and you will quickly discover that answer.

GROWTH VS. OPPORTUNITY

To assemble remarkable teams, not every word needs to be replaced, but some need to be put in their proper place. Without a doubt, every leader wants to experience *growth* in their business. So, unifying their people and creating teams with cohesion and synergy makes complete sense. But most leaders fail to gain the buy-in they had hoped for based on their failure to mention one *keyword*.

I have discovered that people care little for the *growth* of the business when it fails to translate into *opportunity* for them. Many leaders talk endlessly about *growth* – growing the business, growing sales, growing client relationships, growing market share. I know that all of that makes sense and should sound enticing. But moving from Status QUO to Status GROW requires another word.

Leaders are often left feeling frustrated and discouraged after delivering powerful messages to their people about *growth.* But the decision to leave out one word causes a failure to magnetize their people and assemble a remarkable team dedicated to achieving the *growth* they just mentioned.

Remember, we are in the people business and we need to attract people with our words. *Growth* is not a repulsive word, but when we neglect to include *opportunity* in our discussions, *growth* loses its magnetic properties and it fails to pull people together, even for exceptional possibilities.

When I served in the Marine Corps, which is known for its unselfish outlook on the team and an unparalleled focus on troop morale, I learned of an acronym that allowed each of us to know that our leaders were looking out, not just for the accomplishment of the mission, but for the Marines who made up the Marine Corps – W.I.I.F.M.

Pronounced as *wiffem*, it means *What's In It For Me*? In the Marine Corps, we understood the ways that we would experience personal gain in certain scenarios. That could be anything from extended liberty to promotions. It was critical for the mission that each Marine also understood that our leaders had our personal interests in mind.

In business, our team members are thinking about it every time we share ideas about *growth*, whether we speak it or not. They are thinking about it even though they may decide not to ask about it. To unify your people at the highest levels and create unmatched buy-in, assemble a team of remarkable people who have the desire to achieve *growth* and speak about the opportunities in front of them.

Leaders who meticulously outline *growth* without purposefully detailing the *opportunity* for their people miss the *opportunity* to rally the people who will achieve the *growth*. You cannot achieve one without the other. So, let's take a closer look at their definitions:

Growth: a stage in the process of growing; evolution; gradual increase. The size or stage of development.

Opportunity: a favorable juncture of circumstances. a good position for advancement or success and progress; a situation or condition favorable for attainment of a goal.

Never attempt growth without the magnetic appeal of opportunity. Both are needed at the same time. If you want to grow and achieve the goals necessary for success, you need to assemble a remarkable team that understands how the achievements will benefit them, not just the organization. At the media company, we spoke about *growth* consistently but we also connected the growth with the opportunity for the team – future promotions, raises, lateral moves, leadership roles, system enhancements, more territory, new services, and so on.

As we grew, we regularly updated our organizational chart to reflect our current remarkable team. But I always had the next version of the organizational chart posted as well, except this was called our *Opportunity Chart*, detailing future opportunities – the new positions (and departments) needed to support the *growth* we were all striving for.

ASSESS YOUR WORDS

Our words reveal our true character, our intentions, and set the tone for our entire culture, allowing us to assemble remarkable teams. With so much at stake, it does not make sense to allow words to negatively impact our teams and their perceptions.

The words spoken in your environment should *Build Strong Identities, Create Exceptional Attitudes*, and *Assemble Remarkable Teams*. To determine if the words in your environment are delivering their intended impact, take the *Word Assessment* below with your people.

WORD ASSESSMENT

Gauge the tuning of your instruments before attempting to play. Rank each, on a scale of 1-10, 10 being best.

We use magnetic words to attract people   1 2 3 4 5 6 7 8 9 10

Our words impact identity (who we are)   1 2 3 4 5 6 7 8 9 10

Our words help to increase team morale   1 2 3 4 5 6 7 8 9 10

We teach the meaning of our core values   1 2 3 4 5 6 7 8 9 10

Our words unify our people   1 2 3 4 5 6 7 8 9 10

Let's *move* to part II and take a closer look at *The SPEECHES We Share*.

Communication Catalyst

Core Values

Description: Team members will discuss the organization's core values. If core values have not been established, use this exercise to create them.

Time of Exercise: 60 minutes (to discuss core values). More time will be needed to create your core values.

Purpose: To develop a deeper understanding of each core value and learn to speak them more fluently and consistently.

Resources: 3x5 cards, pens, list of core values (some organizations may refer to them as guiding principles, creeds, ethics, etc.).

Presentation:

- Give a 3x5 card and a pen to each participant – one card for each core value.
- Each participant writes the core value at the top of the 3x5 card and what it means to them below. This is a great way to find out if your people know all of your core values.
- Go around and have each participant share their personal definitions of each core value.
- Have an open discussion about each core value and how to have one common definition for the organization.
- Create a list of all core values with their common definitions.

Debrief: Distribute your list of core values and definitions throughout your organization. Share each of them and their definitions during meetings so people become more fluent at speaking them and exemplifying them.

Part II

The SPEECHES We Share

Wise men speak because they have something to say; fools because they have to say something.

~ Plato

Part II

The SPEECHES We Share

Each Speech Sends a Message.

We undoubtedly understand the immense power behind each word we select. Now, as we connect our words, forming sentences, phrases, and dialogue, we increase their magnetic strength. Imagine the untapped potential as we link words together to send our message. Wait a minute, do we send a message every time we speak? Yes! Whether it is planned or not, people are interpreting the ideas behind the connected words we choose to speak - our speeches. Let's look at one definition of *speech*.

Speech: the communication or expression of thoughts in spoken words.

"Talk is cheap." We have all heard this before or perhaps used it ourselves. These three small words send a powerful message when connected. It's meant to convey that it is easier to talk about doing something than to actually do it or that someone does not believe a person will do what they implied in the message from their speech. Some people say it as a response to challenge someone to complete what they just announced.

But is talk actually cheap? Yes! The merit of most dialogue, the worth and value, are often sub-par at best. Speaking combines multiple words to form our conceptual thoughts and we deliver a message, intended or unintended, each time we talk. Most speeches happening in the workplace, short or long, deliberate or spontaneous, often fail to get a return on the investment of time it took to speak the collection of words that were chosen.

Is it possible that people communicate in the workplace without truly understanding the messages they send each time they speak? It happens all too often. After all, talk is cheap, or at least that is the common thought in most workplaces. According to Kat Blackburn, Ph.D., it takes the average person "Approximately 250 milliseconds" to identify a spoken word. People are processing our words nearly as quickly as we verbalize them. But most people put little thought into the impact of their speeches – far less thought than the person hearing and deciphering our message.

Sound Bite:
Each time we speak, we deliver a message to our listeners, whether we intended to or not.

SPEECH CHOICES

The evolution of language has ushered in numerous styles and options for speaking; ways to convey our intended messages. When we talk, we can choose idioms, clichés, and proverbs to emphasize the message behind our speeches. Unfortunately, most people use them without fully understanding the messages they are sending. So, let's take a closer look at some of our choices that impact our speeches and our messages.

An **Idiom** is a phrase or expression that is difficult to understand based on the usual meanings of the words it is derived from.

Example: *We'll cross that bridge when we come to it.*
Message: We'll talk about that problem later.

A **Cliché** is a trite or stereotyped phrase or opinion that is overused and lacks original thought.

Example: *Every cloud has a silver lining.*
Message: You can usually find something good in a bad situation.

A **Proverb** is a short popular saying, usually of unknown origin that states a general truth or wise piece of advice.

Example: *Don't bite the hand that feeds you.*

Message: Don't anger or hurt someone who is helping you.

Our choices do not end there. We can also include adages, epithets, puns, quotations, sayings, witticisms, and many more options. With so much to choose from, misunderstandings and misinterpretations can occur. This is precisely why *communication* is the number one challenge mentioned by most leaders and their team members, in virtually every organization I work with.

But let's take "Communication Issues" one step farther and I'll add that all the other challenges we face are a direct result of some break in *The Communication Movement* with our people. Everything from delegation and accountability to collaboration and planning is affected significantly by our speeches and messages – *the expressions of our thoughts in spoken words.*

Sound Bite:
The connected words we share, our speeches, either build up or tear down morale.

Although we have many choices in how we form our speeches, I have witnessed that they all fall into two distinctive types of dialogue that occur in the workplace. This happens in team meetings and sales meetings, department discussions, and performance evaluations, in training sessions and development classes, in client appointments and casual talks in *team member* lounges. Whether the speech is spoken or written in e-mails and memos, our workplace dialogue sends messages that either prohibits or promotes team cohesion.

The Two Types of Workplace Dialogue:

1. Dividing Dialogue   - prohibits team cohesion
2. Connecting Dialogue   - promotes team cohesion

Talk may be cheap but it is also costly when left to chance; not to choice. So, let's take a closer look at the meaning of both words to better understand the dialogue we need flowing throughout our environments.

Divide: to cause to be separate, disunited, or apart from one another.

Connect: to become joined or fastened. To associate or consider as related.

Dividing dialogue prohibits productivity in the workplace and can result in conflict, frustration, confusion, and an unproductive environment wherein people feel unmotivated and fail to deliver the desired results. Dividing dialogue separates team members, leaders, clients, potential customers, and vendors.

Connecting dialogue promotes productivity and is critical in every workplace culture as an integral component of business success and team cohesion. Connecting dialogue is much more than mitigating conflict and resolving issues. It joins people together and helps to eliminate both before they arise and become consistent and deflating problems.

The impact of dividing dialogue and connecting dialogue are both undeniable. So, let's take a look at some of the impacts they make to determine if you want to pay the price for allowing *Dividing Dialogue* to undermine your people or you are ready to receive a return on investment from *Connecting Dialogue*.

The Impact of DIVIDING Dialogue:

- Low morale
- High stress
- Missed opportunities
- Unmet expectations
- Increased turnover
- Unaccomplished goals
- More mistakes
- Dissatisfied customers
- Sub-par bottom line
- Inconsistent productivity

The Impact of CONNECTING Dialogue:

- High morale
- Strong identity/pride
- New opportunities
- High expectations
- Elevated retention

- Accomplished goals
- Increased efficiencies
- Unsolicited referrals
- Above-par bottom line
- Consistent productivity

While the list can go on and on for both types of communication, I'm sure you're ready to eliminate *Dividing Dialogue* and replace it with *Connecting Dialogue*. *Connecting Dialogue* is *cheaper* than fixing the unnecessary mistakes and low team engagement associated with *Dividing Dialogue*.

WHICH QUADRANT ARE YOU IN?

This book is not your source for becoming better at speaking the English language; it is your resource for becoming fluent at speaking the *Shared Language of Success*, with the intention and purpose of unifying your people. While you may not be a certified professional speaker, I am confident that you speak to people in the workplace. You talk with co-workers, clients, prospects, and vendors. In my book, that qualifies you as a "speaker."

While we are all speakers, how can some people pull others together with their speeches while others push them away? Each time we talk, our dialogue falls into specific quadrants, each generating an impact on the unification of our people – division or connection. The DIALOGUE Quadrant identifies the four outcomes of our speech, positioning us to enhance our dialogue choices, our messages, and our ability to unify people.

The DIALOGUE Quadrant has two categories to identify the impact that speakers make on their audience – anyone who can hear/read their speech and interpret their message. Speakers in the bottom half are known as *Dividers*. Their dialogue creates silos and moves people away from the possibility of teamwork. Speakers in the top half are called *Connectors*. Their dialogue breaks down walls and promotes high levels of teamwork.

Each time you speak, focus on being a connector, not a divider. Very simply, the path to the top half of the quadrant starts with focusing on speaking proactively, to unify others with your message rather than talking reactively, leaving your message to chance and possibly dividing your people. Start with small steps and slowly build up your ability to connect people each time you speak.

The DIALOGUE Quadrant

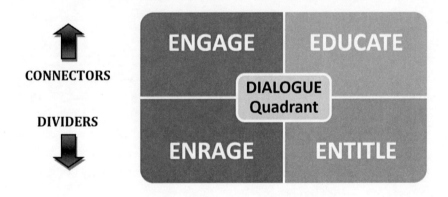

CONNECTORS

Engage: Dialogue that pulls people closer
Educate: Dialogue that builds people up

DIVIDERS

Enrage: Dialogue that pushes people away
Entitle: Dialogue that keeps people down

If you want your people to move from the bottom half of The DIALOGUE Quadrant to the top half, it's time to foster an environment of *Connecting Dialogue.* To ensure that our speeches send the right messages, we are going to fine-tune our communication and focus on the three moving factors that help bring people together.

The Three Moving Factors of our SPEECHES:

1. Vocal Creations Influence
2. Dialogue Inspires Activity
3. Phraseology Fosters Success

Communication Catalyst

Dialogue Quadrant

Description: Identify the "speeches" you hear in the workplace and where each one fits into the *Dialogue Quadrant*.

Time of Exercise: 60 minutes

Purpose: To recognize and discuss the phrases and clichés currently used in your workplace, and the impact they have on people.

Resources: 3x5 cards, pens, white board, white board markers.

Presentation:

- On a whiteboard, list each of the four sections of the Dialogue Quadrant: Engage, Educate, Enrage, Entitle.
- Give a 3x5 card and a pen to each participant.
- Ask participants to list as many phrases or clichés heard in the workplace.
- Go around and have each participant share their phrases and cliches, writing each one in the appropriate quadrant.
- Discuss the perceived meaning of each one as a team.

Debrief: Set up sessions to discuss the *Dialogue Quadrant* with your entire team, identifying the phrases and clichés that are common in your environment. Use this exercise in each department to gain a full understanding of the dialogue flowing through your organization.

Eliminate the "Dividers" and increase the "Connectors."

Chapter 4

Vocal Creations Influence

Most have Noble Intentions but Few Deliver an Impact.

It was halftime during one of my soccer games with the Strikers and it had been a great year so far – we were undefeated. We sat with our Gatorade cups in hand, panting and wiping away the sweat from our faces. Although the score was 3 – 0, we were gathered together with our heads hung low. For the first time this season, we were losing and our chances of a comeback were slim to none, and Slim had just left town. No one said it but each of the Strikers knew the game was over and the pity party was in full swing for every team member. At eleven years old, this would be a devastating loss for each of us.

Our typically loud and overly enthusiastic parents were unusually quiet on the sideline and their silence spoke volumes to us. I glanced at the other side of the field and watched as the opposing players were high-fiving each other as if they had already won the game. Team morale was low, and all hope was gone, or so we thought. Our assistant coach stepped up and knelt by us. He had played soccer in Europe, and in our eyes was a true champion. If only he could put on a jersey and play the second half with us, the Strikers would win for sure.

I discovered that a "win" for our team would not come from his skill on the field but rather his speech at a moment when we needed it the most. He shared the most motivational talk I had ever heard in all of my eleven years. It was probably the only one any of us had ever heard but that still qualifies it as the best. I cannot recall everything he said but I remember how he made us feel. His speech shifted our mindsets and made a huge impact on each of us. The Strikers went back out to the field renewed – rejuvenated.

Could a simple speech make that much of an impact? There were a lot of things he could have said, like "You guys are playing horribly," "They are making you look bad," or "You're a bunch of disappointments." But the words he chose to connect breathed new life into an emotionally defeated team. He said things like, "I believe in each of you" and "They are not better than you, they are just performing better than you, right now." He ended with, "Do you really want it more than they do?" and a few of my fellow players timidly nodded while a few others barely uttered "Yes!"

He said, "What? I can't hear you!" Other Strikers chimed in louder with "Yes!" Then we all started chanting, "Yes! Yes! Yes!" as the halftime came to an end. I looked back over to the other side of the field and the opposing team was no longer high fiving. They were staring at us, and if I interpreted the look on their faces correctly, they were wondering what had just happened to our crushed spirits. It seemed, at least to me, that their confidence had faded.

The Strikers went on to score four unanswered goals. We won! The other team had been shut down by the very same kids that allowed them to score their initial three points during the first half. Our assistant coach's influential speech had lasted only thirty seconds and he did not shout or bark orders at us. He did not put us down or degrade us. Instead, he used his vocal creation to influence us. We may have only been eleven years old but we felt like we had conquered the world when we won that game.

 **Sound Bite:**
It's not the length of your speech that matters, it's the impact of your speech that matters.

EVERY TEAM NEEDS TO HEAR GREAT SPEECHES

If a bunch of eleven-year-olds benefitted from a well-timed motivational speech, imagine the impact it will have on your team. In business, we too can influence the people we work with. But most people are resistant to "motivate" others when they speak. Some act as though these speeches are just a bunch of hype and rah-rah. Remember, the children playing sports, those who are motivated by the right speeches, eventually grow up and go to work in businesses just like yours. While we all thrived off of the powerful dialogue we received as children, we rarely experience it as adults in the workplace. But you can usher *The COMMUNICATION Movement* into your culture with the right vocal creations.

Your team can benefit from powerful messages, just as the Strikers did. While I speak for a living now, I never just "speak." I'm hired to teach people techniques about leadership development, strategic planning, sales excellence, and goal setting. I am always sure to intertwine inspirational messages into every topic, so I can deliver a memorable experience for the audience and increase their retention of my material.

When you speak to your people, do you make an impact? Do they remember the information you just shared? Before I speak, train, or develop an audience, I always conduct a *Discovery Call* with the event planner or some of their leaders to truly understand their team and the challenges they currently face. When I deliver a message, I never want it to be "canned." I strive to be relevant and meaningful to my audience.

After one of my presentations, workshops, webinars, or seminars, it is not uncommon for people to come up to me and say things like, "I needed that" or "I could listen to you all day." While I don't think they want to sit in a room with me for eight hours straight, I do believe that I hit a nerve for that person, typically during the inspirational part of the speech, not just because of the material I was speaking about. When I speak, I search for opportunities to influence people based on where they are in their lives at that moment.

People need powerful, inspirational, and impactful messages in the workplace far more than they will ever ask for, and far more than we will ever know. With all of the benefits of having an inspired, motivated, and enthusiastic team, why is there such a lack of inspiring, motivating, and enthusiastic messages in the workplace? It's quite simple. Too many people feel that it's "not my job." It's not that they are opposed to delivering dynamic messages but they don't believe they are qualified.

Everyone is qualified to influence the people they work with. Period! Perhaps they are not prepared to do it but they are qualified. When I became a member of the NSA (National Speakers Association), I may have acquired the membership but being a member does not mean that I influence others when I speak. It just means that I am a speaker. I must be intentional about influencing every time I speak, or I will merely be talking. We can all decide to do more than just speak. We can intentionally influence others as we deliver our messages.

MOVING SPEECHES LEAVE CLUES

To influence people in the workplace, there is no need to compare ourselves to professional speakers or to try to duplicate some of the greatest speeches ever made. No one is expecting you to be the next Gandhi or Martin Luther King Jr. at your next meeting. But we can learn from them. When we think about great speakers and their famous speeches, we tend to look back into history to find some of the most endearing and inspiring collection of words ever assembled.

These speeches delivered powerful messages that shaped nations and brought about much-needed enhancements (not change) in our world. They empowered people to stay strong during challenging times and encouraged them to take action when they felt defeated. Below is a list of twelve speakers and their speeches, spanning over 1,500 years.

Twelve of the Greatest Speeches in History:

1. Jesus Christ   – The Sermon on the Mount
2. Winston Churchill   – Their Finest Hour
3. Demosthenes   – The Third Philippic (342 B.C.)
4. Frederick Douglass   – Fighting Rebels With Only One Hand
5. Mary Fisher   – A Whisper of AIDS

6. Mahatma Gandhi   – Quit India
7. Lou Gehrig   – Farewell to baseball address
8. John F. Kennedy   – The Decision to Go to the Moon
9. Martin Luther King Jr. – I Have a Dream
10. Abraham Lincoln   – The Gettysburg Address
11. Ronald Reagan   – Address to the Nation on the Challenger
12. Anna Howard Shaw   – Fundamental Principle of a Republic

I know what you're thinking, "I'm not trying to save the world, free a country, or even encourage people to rise up against oppression." While you are one hundred percent correct, I'm sure that you would appreciate your people fully understanding what you say and becoming more excited to take action every time you speak. These famous speeches, like dozens of other well-known speeches, share some common elements that we can all use to deliver our messages more effectively when we speak to our people

Sound Bite:
Our vocal creations have the power to deliver hope and increase the engagement in those who hear them.

The twelve vocal creations above had the power to influence people, regardless of their circumstances. Just as our assistant coach did at halftime, for the eleven-year-old Strikers, we can all enhance our speeches by taking a closer look at the four common elements that each speech contained. When combined, these factors allow us to deliver a message that unifies and connects people.

The Four Factors of a GREAT Speech:

1. Address the *Challenge*
2. Announce the *Solution*
3. Share the *Vision*
4. Provide the *Inspiration*

Each great speech may reveal these four qualities in a different order but they are there, intentionally combined to create the desired result. When my role was the vice president of the media company, I used these elements each time I spoke to our entire team, each department, and our people individually. I never just spoke. I always searched for ways to influence people to be their best and to overcome their current challenges. I use them now, as a professional speaker, to ensure that my message is memorable and impactful. You have this opportunity, too.

Every time you talk with your people, you can influence them. You possess the ability to share a message they may desperately need. Never underestimate the power of your vocal creations in your day-to-day work environment. Do not feel the need to deliver your message in the styles of graduation commencements, inaugural addresses, or annual event keynotes each time you speak. In the workplace, your vocal creations will be shorter in length and much more impromptu but can still pack an influential punch during each meeting, conference call, or one-to-one encounter with your people.

MOVING SPEAKERS LEAVE HOPE

Impactful speakers show a better place, then describe how to get there. They share their vision then detail the steps required to arrive. In the workplace, I have discovered that most people leave out the key elements required to influence their people and then wonder why their talk or their speech fell flat. Most leaders talk only about the steps to get somewhere – what needs to be done. They neglect to address the vision and provide the inspiration required to influence their audience. We cannot afford to think, "It's not my job," when it comes to these two factors.

Delivered from the Lincoln Memorial in Washington D.C. to over 250,000 people, Martin Luther King Jr. powerfully shared, "I have a dream" about halfway into his famous speech, on August 28, 1963. When he chose the word *dream*, he conveyed the understanding that it hasn't happened yet; it is in the future. His vision and his belief level helped to inspire his audience to take the actions required to realize his dream. He gave them hope.

Martin Luther King Jr.'s speech lasted just over sixteen minutes but he provided enough inspiration to move his dream forward. After his speech at the feet of Lincoln, both the passage of the landmark Civil Rights Act of 1964 and the Voting Rights Act of 1965 were accomplished. In the workplace, some people speak much longer than sixteen minutes in their daily meetings but they often say far less. Again, it's not the length of your speech, it's the magnitude of your impact.

When we speak to people at work, we need to move away from the notion that we are trying to deliver a speech that is going to enhance the world. We also need to acknowledge that the challenges we face in the workplace are nowhere near the level of the challenges faced by the twelve speakers mentioned earlier. But we can borrow factors from each of them. To unify our people, we can all address a current *challenge*, announce a *solution*, and share the *vision* for a better future. Wait! That's only three of the four factors. You are correct!

Let's talk about the fourth factor for a moment - *inspiration*. We also need to provide the *inspiration* our people need to get the mission accomplished with the best attitudes possible. If you were to write out a speech, you could have a few paragraphs addressing the *challenge*, a detailed plan for the *solution*, and a couple of sections dedicated to your *vision*. But you cannot merely write in *inspiration*.

"Insert Inspiration Here" is not going to make the inspiration occur. The speaker is the key to delivering the message and is the source of the inspiration needed to make it a reality. To connect with their audience, *unifying* speakers combine three important qualities when they speak.

The Three Qualities of an Inspirational Speaker (S³):

1. Substance
2. Style
3. Structure

SUBSTANCE

Content is king. Is your topic relevant to your audience? When you speak, you must do more than talk - your exchange of information must emotionally touch your audience. As you are preparing what you want to discuss, make sure it is meaningful to them. If you are addressing a challenge, make sure the solution is presented, too. Be sure to have facts, data, and resources to support your speech. Know your material.

STYLE

The *way* you speak can make or break your message. As important as what you are talking about, your delivery conveys a significant message to your audience. Before you speak, get in the zone – the mental state to share your *substance* with the highest levels of confidence, belief, enthusiasm, and when appropriate, add humor. Your style translates into relatability and relatability allows people to embrace the substance you share.

STRUCTURE

Too many people incorrectly feel that structuring their speeches takes away from the genuine and sincere impact they are striving for. When we fail to structure the order of our delivery, we miss opportunities to make a greater impact. First, begin by having an outcome for your speech. Next, break it into three parts – the introduction (of your outcome), the main body (of your substance), and the conclusion (of your impact). The structure allows the audience to fully understand your intended message.

I have used these three qualities to achieve success in both the financial services industry and the media industry. Now, as a professional speaker, I never take the stage and hope for the best. I pay close attention to the substance of my speeches, my style, and how I structure them.

SPEAKING IS POWER

While public speaking may be one of our greatest fears, it is also our greatest tool in the workplace. Unfortunately, it is highly underutilized. Most people speak in response to a question or to address an issue. They are reactionary with their speeches. We need to proactively speak to influence. Language impacts people, significantly altering moods, behaviors, and emotions, which in turn, impacts performance, effectiveness, and results. Our speeches, short or long, rehearsed or spontaneous, have tremendous power.

In the words of Peter Parker's uncle, "With great power comes great responsibility." While Spiderman used his powers to fight crime, great speakers use their powers to fight the status quo. Every time we speak, we have the *power* to influence the way people feel and the actions they take. We can move people from, "Here's how it's always been done," to "Here's what we can do!" A moving speech can come from anyone, at any time, and range in any duration. It can last an hour, a few minutes, or just seconds.

When we intentionally connect our words, anything is possible. Just like in sports, creating high levels of engagement and motivation in the workplace is crucial for accelerating the achievements of our team members. But most people do not think they are cut out to deliver dialogue that motivates others, especially in the workplace. They often choose silence, thus closing the window of opportunity to influence others. With engagement and productivity levels lower than desired in most businesses, an empowering speech can be the catalyst for a positive shift in the mindsets of your people.

 **Sound Bite:**
Every time we speak, we open the window of opportunity to influence others.

I have to think that at least some of the 250,000 people listening to Martin Luther King Jr.'s speech, had some trepidation and concern about the *dream* he shared, no matter how powerful it was. With hundreds of years of slavery and oppression on their minds, is it possible some may have thought, "I like his speech but this is how it's always been?" While we cannot force anyone to be motivated, excited, enthusiastic, or positive, we can, and do, influence people every time we speak.

Our speeches directly impact the mood of the team. We can feel it when morale is high and we can feel it when it is low. In both cases, the power source, to either lift people up or tear them down, is linked to the influence of our dialogue. A pay raise, a free lunch, or some trophies may provide a positive spike in morale but is usually just a temporary fix. It is often the words from a colleague, a co-worker, or a leader that will deliver the long-lasting inspiration needed to influence someone's thoughts and actions.

At the media company, I may have started as an entry-level scheduler but when I spoke, I transformed into the CIO – Chief Influence Officer. I added small doses of impact when I talked. I did not cave in to the negativity, gossip, or undermining discussions that were already hurting our culture. I began to connect my words wisely to begin the process of influencing my fellow team members. I may have been the new guy, and at the bottom of the Org Chart, but I sent a message to my co-workers every time I spoke.

As the new guy, I was not leading any meetings, conducting hiring interviews, or providing training sessions. My speeches were short and sweet, filled with magnetic words, and laced together with positivity. I tried to deliver a powerful message every time I spoke with another team member. Were my vocal creations well-received by everyone? No, not at first. There was some resistance but that only proved the need for better communication in our environment.

I began to select, and connect, magnetic words to send powerful messages. When there was a mistake, I stopped the finger-pointing by saying, "This is a great opportunity to enhance our systems and our training." If people became discouraged due to an equipment malfunction, I announced, "What a perfect time to revisit our maintenance schedule." If someone quit and others needed to shoulder their workload, I said, "I'm looking forward to having a new person join our team."

It is all too common that most people save their "inspiring" speeches for "crunch" time – when there is a looming timeline (not deadline) that is about to be missed, an upcoming appointment with a key account that still needs some vital prep work, or a major mistake occurred and the entire team is in recovery mode to retain a valued client. Times like these require motivation but we do not need to wait until motivation is desperately needed, to influence on a regular basis.

By understanding the four factors of great speeches and the three qualities of inspirational speakers, we can choose our word combinations more thoughtfully, more intentionally, and more impactfully. One of the biggest problems with communication in the workplace is the lack of thought put into the words flowing out of people's mouths. Their intention often fails to match the meaning pouring into people's ears.

 **Sound Bite:**
The message delivered is infinitely more impactful than words spoken.

Your team does not need to wait for the next motivational speaker to take the stage at an annual event to influence them. You are in front of them more than any professional speaker and you can deliver a powerful message every time you speak to them if you are prepared to raise the bar. Wait! Did I just use a cliché? Not hardly. You'll see.

RAISE THE BAR

"Four score and..." well, you know the rest. "seven years ago." Most people today have no clue what Abraham Lincoln was referring to when he mentioned *score* in his famous speech, but people recall the beginning of the *Gettysburg Address*. He chose *score* because it was a widely known measure of time, meaning "20 years." Today, he would simply state "87 years ago."

Fortunately, we do not need to focus on creating our own *Gettysburg Address* or *I Have a Dream* speech each time we talk in the workplace but we should possess situational awareness of our word combinations. When it comes to influencing people as we speak, it's time to *raise the bar*. Ok, let's tackle this phrase before we move onto other powerful sayings that support *The COMMUNICATION Movement* in your business.

I have attended more meetings than I can count. Maybe you can relate. To boost morale, get people-focused, and set the stage for success, it is common to hear people say, "It's time to raise the bar." The feeling of raw enthusiasm and unbridled energy courses through the entire audience for about 3.8 seconds. After a few nods of approval, the "bar" is never mentioned again, not just during the speech but when people return to work.

So, why say it in the first place? Why buy a car if you never intend on driving it? Like all phrases, people say them with the best of intentions. Unfortunately, they often fail to harness the power they yield. They use sayings to switch perceptions but when they fail to follow through on them, they miss the opportunity to ignite the inspiration in their people. We can no longer ignore the meaning and the message behind each phrase, saying, and cliché used in the workplace.

While most people will say that the biggest problem with clichés, like "Raise the Bar," is that they are overused, I couldn't disagree more. They are unfortunately *underused*. Let me elaborate. As a business coach, I have attended meetings and heard people enthusiastically proclaim, "Let's raise the bar" and as expected, morale elevates momentarily.

After the meetings, I ask, "What bar are you going to raise?" With a bewildered look, they reply, "What do you mean?" I answer with, "Well, you mentioned raising the bar, so which bar did you have in mind?" My question is typically followed by head-scratching silence, so I quickly add, "Does your team know what bar to raise?" Again, more silence. So, I add, "Ok, never mind which bar you meant. What level are you raising it to?" As you can imagine, neither the bar nor the level is clearly articulated. The inspiration was switched on but not fully ignited. Again, this powerful saying loses its full power in about 3.8 seconds.

It's time to raise the *Communication Bar* each time we speak. Now that you're reading this book, you possess this bar. But how do we know it's a communication bar? Simple, it says *Communication Bar* on it. It also has our name on it – we own it. But everyone uses it differently when they speak. Some lower it (*poor* communication) while others disrupt people with it (*turbulent* communication). Some set it down and do nothing with it (*missing* communication).

We must raise it (*influential* communication) together. Note that the *Communication Bar* is wider than our two hands, so we should invite others to help raise it with us as they speak, too. Using well-crafted vocal creations to influence people, others will begin to duplicate us. Imagine what your environment would feel like if everyone thought about sending a powerful message before they spoke. So, let's take a closer look at where to start.

Understanding the influential possibilities of our dialogue is a powerful start. But to experience the benefits of this communication movement, you and your team will need to raise the *Communication Bar* consistently. *The Speeches we Share* will be enhanced as we use our vocal creations to influence those around us.

Over the next two chapters, we will take a look at common phrases used in the workplace, and learn how to integrate them into our dialogue, or eliminate them from our dialogue, with a clear understanding and a deeper meaning, so our vocal creations can deliver greater influence.

Communication Catalyst

Create a Speech

Description: Create a powerful message that addresses an issue, using the *Four Factors of a GREAT Speech*.

Time of Exercise: 60 minutes

Purpose: To become familiar with planning out a speech or discussion, especially to resolve or eliminate a problem.

Resources: White board, white board markers.

Presentation:

- Ask participants to list specific challenges that exist in the workplace.
- Choose one challenge to target and identify as many solutions as possible to resolve/eliminate it.
- As a team, create a message that announces the challenge and its solutions.
- Incorporate the vision of your company into the message.
- Identify ways to inspire the entire team and add them into the speech.
- Rehearse the delivery of the message – each person taking a turn to share the speech in a dynamic way.

Debrief: Continue to "Drill for Skill" with every speech that you create for each individual challenge. Become comfortable delivering inspiring messages to address challenging topics.

Chapter 5

Dialogue Inspires Activity

Adding New Meaning to Old Sayings.

When people tell you to 'break a leg' they don't really mean it. At least I hope not. Unfortunately, they also do not mean most of the other common catchphrases they say in the workplace, like "let's raise the bar," "we need to speak the same language," "let's give it 110%," "we need to be on the same page," "let's hit the ground running," "push the envelope," "move the needle," or "think outside of the box." The list goes on and on.

People choose clever wording material every day in their work environments to help convey their messages. Most, however, fail to provide a clear understanding of the meaning behind the expression; a meaning that is shared by their entire team. When we communicate, our dialogue choices guide our people, encouraging them to either follow us or to abandon us. Most people use popular sayings but fail to deliver their intended impact. I hear business professionals add well-known terminology to their speeches that could deliver tremendous power but often fizzle out too early.

I'm not opposed to working in a good-old-fashioned cliché, phrase, or saying but haphazardly choosing a remark, which could be easily misunderstood and misinterpreted will have a devastating impact on your message. When someone says, "Let's give 110%," then heads straight out to lunch, the meaning is diminished. Our dialogue choices assist in the bonding process of our teams – either moving people closer together or pushing them farther apart. Making GREAT dialogue choices provide us with opportunities to unify our people and unlock their true potential.

Today, numerous articles are emphasizing the avoidance of clichés, phrases, and sayings. But that's purely based on the second phase of the dialogue not occurring. Hey wait, there are phases? Yes, every time we share our dialogue, it comes in two possible phases. Possible? Yes, they are possible – possible to achieve both and possible not to achieve both. You want to achieve both!

The Two Phases of Our Phrases:

1. **The Dialogue Switch:** The initial impact. The rush of enthusiasm, and the emotional response felt when a specific part of your speech (cliché, phrase, or saying) is mentioned.

   ‣ Your Dialogue Switch inspires people!

2. **The Dialogue Light**: The after effect. The moment "the light bulb turns on" and your message is interpreted (meaning and intention), causing the desire to take action.

   ‣ Your Dialogue Light guides people!

I can often detect when members of my audience experience a *dialogue switch* – I may have said something that delivered relevant and timely meaning to them. When the switch is flipped, it creates a physical reaction in people. They may adjust their body language by leaning in or nodding their heads. Some take copious notes while others lean over and repeat the phrase to their neighbor. They just experienced an "aha moment" when the *dialogue switch* was flipped.

One of my favorite and most popular Think GREAT sayings is, "Leadership is the... " and everyone replies with "the people business." I love seeing audiences react to the switch but that lasts only 3.8 seconds unless I can add fuel to the meaning and purpose. After the flip of the switch, I need to deliver the message that creates the light required to guide them in a new direction – to take action. I show them techniques to empower and build people – I back up my sayings with strategy.

When people speak and no one takes action, they have either failed to flip the switch, see the light, or both. Just as a lighter allows us to light a candle, our dialogue choices must position us to deliver both the Switch (inspiration) and the Light (guidance). Lighters were not designed to merely create a small flame for a momentary flicker. They were created to transfer the energy from one source to another source – to light something. When we use a cliché, a phrase, or a saying, without any follow-through message, it is like rolling the metal wheel of a lighter with our thumb (flicking the switch) and being satisfied with the switch but doing nothing with the small flame (using the light).

Sound Bite:
When you choose your dialogue, prepare to deliver both the switch and the light required for action.

When we intentionally interject a common expression into our dialogue, we intend to flip the switch. Unfortunately, most "speakers" flip switches each day but do the proverbial "mic drop" afterward and fail to follow through with the light needed to guide the pathway to action. Unleashing the positive effects of our message happens after we say it, not as we say it. Remember, the switch (Phase 1) occurs when we say something but the light (Phase 2) only occurs when we deliver on it.

You now have the opportunity to strengthen *The Communication Movement* in your organization as you harness the power of known sayings, phrases, and clichés, many of which are already being used by you and your people. Like all of our dialogue choices, we need to take a close look at their unification potential. Do they bond your people or separate them? After all, "You catch more flies with honey than with vinegar!"

OUR DIALOGUE CHOICES CREATE AN EXPERIENCE

There are too many clichés, phrases, and sayings to list in one chapter. Regardless of which one is chosen, they are all accompanied by a series of interpretations, feelings, and sensations that either help or hurt your message. The dialogue switch is experienced emotionally but when it fails to create the light needed for action, it falls flat. Instead of fueling the long-lasting inspiration needed for success, underused sayings may build up high-levels of resentment and frustration.

Below are popular phrases used in the workplace. When we do little more than "flip" the switch, each of them can deliver confusion, misunderstandings, and misinterpretations.

Popular Phrases and their Unintentional Side Effects:

- **Let me be honest!**
  Have you been dishonest?

- **My door is always open!**
  Did you really just authorize me to jump the chain of command?

- **Failure is not an option!**
  Well, it actually is, and I've experienced failure here before.

- **It's a win-win situation!**
  It sounds like we have not won anything yet.

- **Think outside the box!**
  Are you implying that I'm stuck inside the box?

- **Push the envelope!**
  Where is this magic envelope? And where am I pushing it to?

- **The data never lies!**
  But I have seen data interpreted and manipulated before, in many ways.

- **Drink the Kool-Aid!**

Stop this one immediately! It makes me think about the 900+ people who died when cult leader, Jim Jones, convinced his followers to drink poisoned Flavor-Aid and Kool-Aid.

- **Value-added!**
  Are you sending me grocery shopping?

- **Grab the low-hanging fruit!**
  Did you just compare the importance of our projects, goals, objectives, and expectations to a piece of fruit? Fruit can rot, correct?

- **Let's peel back the layers of the onion!**
  Am I going to cry during this? And why so many produce references?

- **Take it to the next level!**
  Are we in an arcade? I'm having Super Mario Bros flashbacks!

- **Here's my 2 cents...**
  Is the worth of your insights so little?

- **Put your ducks in a row!**
  I am picturing baby duckies following their mama across the street.

- **Let's put lipstick on this pig!**
  Ok, another farm animal reference... and is our project, product, or offering comparable to swine?

- **I know you've been burning the candle at both ends!**
  Sounds like you're getting ready to give me more work.

- **We need to move the needle!**
  Am I authorized to use medical equipment?

- **It's basic blocking and tackling!**
  So you're telling me I can't screw this up?

- **Let's put our game faces on!**
  What? Are there visual examples for me to see?

- **Step up to the plate!**
  Oh, ok, more sports metaphors.

- **I need to pick your brain!**
  Is there a zombie apocalypse I should be aware of?

- **Let's take a 30,000-foot view!**
  Am I unable to understand this from the ground?

- **I want you to run with this!**
  Are you tossing me onto the street and expecting me to figure it out on my own?

Do I use some of these sayings? Absolutely. Have you? Probably. I have nothing against them when they "light" the inspiration required for action. These phrases, and many of my other favorite dialogue choices, are great ways to increase engagement when you speak. When used properly, they can encourage imaginations to soar and excitement to rise. But when we fail to activate both phases, and no action occurs, some people may say that our dialogue choices "leave a bad taste in my mouth."

DIALOGUE FLAVORS

When people are asked how something tastes, they could easily choose words like "bad" or "delicious." But if they want to get more detailed, they can select a specific number of ways to describe their taste sensations. While there is some discussion about the actual number of tastes we experience, there are five universally accepted basic tastes that result from a chemical reaction between stimuli (food) and the receptors in our mouths (taste buds).

The five basic tastes are sweet, salty, sour, bitter, and umami. Umami is a Japanese word (旨味) and refers to a savory taste. Often translated as "deliciousness," it is also known to mean a "pleasant taste" or "essence." Understanding how to describe our desired taste allows us to prepare meals that deliver the desired outcome. Imagine for a moment, if our dialogue captures the "essence" of our intended meaning, purpose, intent, and message.

Unfortunately, when it comes to our sense of hearing, we do not have basic categories to interpret what we hear, as we do when it comes to our sense of taste. This is precisely why there is such a drastic disconnect in the workplace and communication is ranked as one of the top challenges in most organizations – internally with team members and externally with customers.

Sound Bite:
People decipher everything we say, just as our taste buds interpret everything we eat.

When a sweet message is interpreted as sour, the reaction is far from what we expect. Just think of a baby's face when he is unexpectedly given a spoon full of lemon juice, especially if he was anticipating the sweet taste of apple juice. It certainly affects his mood and body language, among many other things. Ok, so it makes for some pretty funny videos but eventually, the baby will be hesitant to take more spoonfuls from his parents if the disconnect continues. A lack of trust will be built up unless the flavor is switched.

ASSESSING YOUR DIALOGUE

We rely heavily on our hearing to interpret and understand our surroundings. In the workplace, our ability to hear others is paramount to our ability to accomplish tasks, fulfill our mission, and achieve our desired results. But hearing is just one thing – understanding is everything. Hearing starts with your ears but understanding happens in your mind.

As English writer Thomas Fuller once stated, "You cannot make sweet wine with sour grapes." With so much riding on the communication happening in the workplace, it makes sense to assess the unification qualities of our dialogue. Hearing dialogue and understanding dialogue are rarely the same things. We have all heard someone speak but not understood what they were saying. When there is confusing dialogue, it's not uncommon to hear people say things like, "Where's she going with this?" We may have heard each word spoken but the meaning was lost as people connected the words from her speech.

If only there was a way to describe the dialogue choices happening in the workplace like there are to describe our sense of taste. There is! It starts with the basic steps required for people to hear our dialogue. Without getting too deep into the physiology of hearing, there are six basic steps that allow us to hear. This is the very abbreviated version.

Step 1:   Sound waves arrive at the tympanic membrane.

Step 2:   Movement of the membrane displaces the auditory ossicles.

Step 3:   The stapes at the oval window applies pressure waves.

Step 4:   Pressure waves move to the round window of the tympanic duct.

Step 5:   Vibration of the basilar membrane causes vibrations of hair cells.

Step 6:   Information travels to the Central Nervous System.

Our sense of hearing is a remarkable process but it does not explain how we transfer sound waves into meaning – how the switch and the light are understood. For that, another step is required – the seventh step.

Step 7:   Dialogue "waves" *magnetize* our interpretations, either unifying or repelling our desire to take action.

Yes, this is a step that is only found and taught in *The Communication Movement*. It is not found in medical journals, although it is happening in every one of us throughout every conversation we are part of. Steps 1-6 allow us to hear the switch. Step 7 allows us to see the light.

Sound Bite:
When you speak, ensure that people not only hear you but also allow them to understand you.

Our challenge, when communicating, is not the ability of our audience to hear us. The first six steps ensure that they can do that. The real challenge is always, do they understand us? In a world of diminishing attention spans, we must ensure that the interpretation of our message happens quickly – the switch of inspiration must rapidly lead to the light of guidance.

When we measure acoustic sound, we use decibel levels to describe the intensity of the volume we experience. It is an easy determination of loudness that uses an actual scale, ranging from 0db to 140dB – the decibel scale.

DECIBEL SCALE (dB)

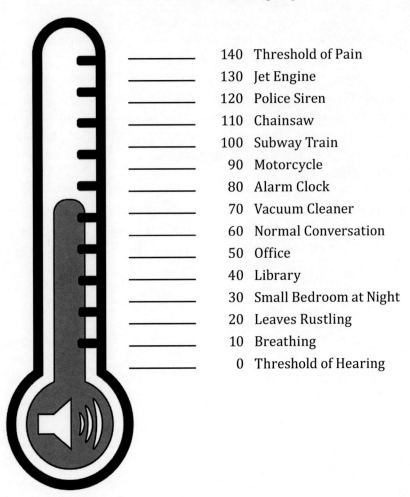

140	Threshold of Pain
130	Jet Engine
120	Police Siren
110	Chainsaw
100	Subway Train
90	Motorcycle
80	Alarm Clock
70	Vacuum Cleaner
60	Normal Conversation
50	Office
40	Library
30	Small Bedroom at Night
20	Leaves Rustling
10	Breathing
0	Threshold of Hearing

The decibel scale allows us to measure the volume of sound. But because our communication is intangible, there is no exact science to measure the impact it has on any one person. So, I created the Delivery Scale to gauge the impact of our dialogue, describing the experience we are likely to have on the individual hearing our conversations. Using a scale of 0 to 100, the mid-range of 50 represents conversations that are a basic transference of information.

When you say something and your instructions were understood, you ranked a 50. You transferred information and you did not lean toward unifying or repelling. Each of us can transfer information with varying levels of unification and repulsion mixed in. Just because we may not rank its impact, does not mean that it is not felt.

We must all be aware of the power of our dialogue choices. Strive to be in the top half of the scale, with the goal of ranking 100 as often as possible.

DELIVERY SCALE (dV)

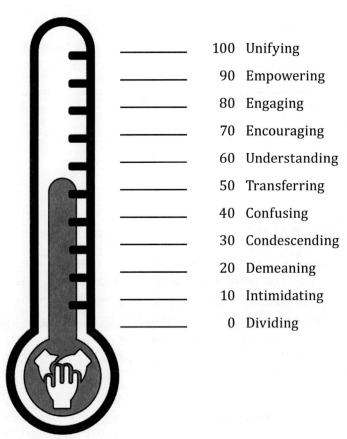

100	Unifying
90	Empowering
80	Engaging
70	Encouraging
60	Understanding
50	Transferring
40	Confusing
30	Condescending
20	Demeaning
10	Intimidating
0	Dividing

The delivery scale allows us to measure the correlation between our dialogue and our desired results – goals, objectives, and projects. When we strive to provide a positive experience from the top half of the Delivery Scale, we inspire the action required for success. Possessing a situational awareness of our dialogue choices will position us to inspire and guide those who hear us. When we fail to choose our dialogue wisely, we may unintentionally find our impact in the lower half of the Delivery Scale.

When we deliver on the switch, using a catchy phrase, saying, or cliché, without an understood and a shared message to ignite the light, the impact can be devastating. To ensure that we rank higher on the Delivery Scale, and create the actions needed for success, we must always focus on transforming our dialogue – the phrases we choose. Before we share our selected saying with our people, we need to strive to transform them by paying close attention to three specific outcomes.

Three Dialogue Transformers:

1. Explain the meaning
2. Create the buy-in
3. Achieve the results

EXPLAIN THE MEANING

Every time we speak, we exchange information, feelings, and meaning. Instead of randomly choosing a common catchphrase, select the saying that is most relevant to the context of your discussion. If you opt for, "Let's raise the bar," you must explain what bar you are referring to, what level you are raising it to, who is helping to raise the bar, when the bar should be fully raised, and anything else to convey what the end state looks like – your outcome.

Sound Bite:
When you share a catchphrase, back it up with all of the details needed to bring it to life – to add meaning.

CREATE THE BUY-IN

When our dialogue choices fall flat, we hinder engagement and actions in those who hear us. Creating high levels of *buy-in* is our desired intent, every time we speak, but it is a two-step process. Our dialogue *switch* allows us to receive *agreement* from our people like, "Yes, we do need to raise the bar." But it is the buy-in from our people that will allow the light to come on, and in this case, to guarantee that the bar is raised enthusiastically – "How can I help to raise the bar?"

Sound Bite:
When people understand the true intention of our dialogue, we create high levels of buy-in.

ACHIEVE THE RESULTS

Follow-through is the key to transforming dialogue into actions – results. It's not the clichés people dislike, it's the unachieved potential. Without follow-through, results are merely a dream, and team members begrudgingly reply to the cliché with their own – "Here we go again." The achievements of the desired results provide everyone involved with a sense of accomplishment and purpose. Most importantly, our dialogue choice was not hot air – it was the catalyst for success.

Sound Bite:
When we achieve the results detailed in our dialogue, more people want to hear our next dialogue choice.

WE REAP WHAT WE SOW

It is easy to think about workplace dialogue as simple conversations between two or more people but it is much more, with unlimited possibilities. To flip the switch and create action, we must deliver our messages without bias or ego, speaking without judging, and encouraging dialogue to flow back and forth. We must ensure an environment of empowering *dialogue* not self-serving *monologue.* Every speech has power!

speech

noun

- the power of expressing or communicating thoughts by speaking.
- the expression of or the ability to express thoughts and feelings by articulate sounds.
- an address or discourse delivered to an audience.
- something that is spoken.

Workplace interactions are vital to teamwork, so we cannot take our dialogue choices lightly. Not only do they build and maintain relationships, but the phrases spoken in the workplace foster everything from innovation and solutions to engagement and morale. Most importantly, our dialogue choices help to break down silos and barriers, set the precedents for communication expectations, and develop the mutual respect needed for forward momentum.

Each time we speak, our dialogue has the potential to paint the picture of unlimited growth or the image of limited stagnation. Poorly selected dialogue choices spread like the streaks of old paint on your canvas, slowly diminishing the possibilities of team cohesion and unification. A communication *streak* is an issue that will only become more evident with time. Right now, is the best time to make GREAT dialogue choices; to paint a picture that inspires the desire for action.

Sound Bite:
Your communication painting should inspire and move people to take action.

Remember, no matter what industry you work in, you are always in the people business, and our dialogue choices make the workplace more human. The stakes are too high to leave our dialogue choices to chance. A failure to create *The COMMUNICATION Movement* in your work environment can put you at a serious disadvantage. The potential impact of misinterpretations and misunderstandings is too much to ignore. Making the right dialogue choices will not only help reinforce that our message is heard but it will reinforce meaningful two-way conversations.

In the next chapter, we are going to look at the language required for high levels of consistent success.

Communication Catalyst

Cliché Busters

Description: Identify clichés used in the workplace and breakdown their true meaning.

Time of Exercise: 60 minutes

Purpose: To identify regularly used phrases in the workplace and how to properly explain them.

Resources: 3x5 cards, pens, white board, white board markers.

Presentation:

- Give a 3x5 card and a pen to each participant.
- Ask participants to list as many clichés as possible in 5 minutes.
- Go around and have each participant share their clichés.
- Each person writes down the clichés mentioned and their meaning.
- Have an open discussion of how to explain the meaning of each cliché to anyone who may hear it.
- Create a final list of all the acceptable clichés in your workplace environment and what their true meanings are.

Debrief: Encourage all leaders to do this exercise with their people to develop a deeper meaning of the phrases and clichés being used. Identify the clichés that should be allowed and those that should be removed.

Chapter 6

Phraseology Fosters Success

Pick Your Side.

"To be successful, you have to have your heart in your business and your business in your heart." While I wholeheartedly agree with this quote from Thomas Watson Sr., I want to emphasize that your heart cannot do the job alone – it requires another biological feature – your mouth. Our workplace language helps to foster an environment for success and makes the biggest impact on the performance of our people. When I say *language*, I'm not referring to English, Spanish, or German. I am speaking about implementing the *Shared Language of Success*.

Low engagement levels in the workplace are a clear sign that most people do not have their "hearts in the business," and it's fair to say that the current phraseology is likely sub-par. According to Gallup, "The percentage of workers who are 'actively disengaged' - those who have miserable work experiences and spread their unhappiness to their colleagues is 14%." They added that an additional "54% of workers are 'not engaged' - they are psychologically unattached to their work and company."

Unattached? Miserable? Are these words in their job descriptions? No! Yet, these are the specific *words* Gallup chose to describe this workplace epidemic. Worse yet, these "employees" use their communication skills to *spread* their unhappiness to other members of their teams. They are undeniably disconnected, lacking any semblance of cohesion or unity. That's 68% of the workplace that does not have their heart in <u>your</u> business. Worse yet, they use their voices to influence others, even though they may work for leaders who have their *hearts in the business*. When it comes to your organization, the voice is more powerful than the heart!

Amazingly, 68% of the workforce is not fully engaged but they are fully paid – they receive 100% of their wages but deliver far less than 100% of their expectations. What is the likelihood of achieving success with this type of investment? That's easy to answer. There is a 0% return on investment when there is little to no engagement in the majority of your people. As Hamlet would probably say in this scenario, if he were a business leader, "To be engaged or not to be engaged? That is the question."

WORKPLACE ENGAGEMENT LEVELS

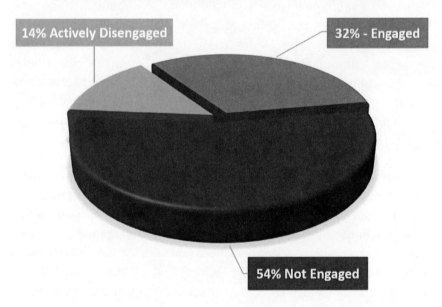

It is time to pick your side. Yes, there are two sides – engagement and non-engagement. It is time to expand the percentage of engaged team members in your workplace. With 68% falling into the "non-engaged" sections, that leaves just under one-third of the workforce who are "engaged." They can deliver the results required to fulfill the mission and achieve the vision of your business but they are significantly outnumbered - hindered and hampered by the other 68%.

This situation is both frustrating and frightening to be stuck in. Non-engagement is the side effect of lackluster language. How important is the link between communication and engagement? I'm glad you asked. According to the article, *Role of Communication in Employee Engagement* by the media company, People Matters, they state that "Communication is a powerful tool that can have an enormous impact on the success of any organization. Effective communication can increase employee engagement, boost workplace productivity, and drive business growth. Communication is the cornerstone of an engaged workforce."

This is precisely why we need to introduce dialogue that delivers encouragement, engagement, empowerment, and unification – the top half of the *Delivery Scale*. We need a language that fosters consistent success. As the Czech proverb so profoundly states, "Learn a new language and get a new soul." Every business benefits when people do more than just show up for eight hours. Organizations benefit when people speak a shared language during those hours, allowing them to unleash their soul (their spirit) in the workplace.

 **Sound Bite:**
To increase engagement, speak a language that entices people to open their hearts and share their souls in your business.

True success occurs when everyone puts their *heart* and *soul* into their work and uses their mouths to speak in a way that uplifts people, boosts their mindsets, and enhances the workplace. You must wage a war against non-engagement because those who fall into that category tend to verbalize their unhappiness far more than your engaged team members verbalize their happiness.

HOW IMPORTANT ARE YOUR ENGAGED PEOPLE?

Now, let's further discuss the 32% – the "engaged." Supporting our team members in this category is mission-critical. We must create an environment that inspires them to maintain their positive attitudes and motivates them to consistently speak in a way that sets the example for the entire team. To do that, understand that the 32% are not all at the same level of engagement. I like to break it up into three different levels.

The Three Levels of Engagement:

- Somewhat Engaged
- Mostly Engaged
- Highly Engaged

Somewhat Engaged – Situational

These people perform well in a team setting and try their best to deflect the negativity and pessimism from the other 68%. Their attitudes are typically good but their engagement level rises and falls based on the circumstances they face. They sometimes cross the line between *engaged* and *not-engaged* causing their attitudes to be perceived as slightly non-engaged.

▸ They exhibit *situational* engagement.

Mostly Engaged – Intentional

These people thrive in a team environment and consistently can be trusted to wholeheartedly embrace positive messages. The 68% tend to annoy those in this category, causing them to partake in the conflict that will arise when engaged and non-engaged team members cross paths. They maintain an above-average level of enthusiasm and excitement the majority of the time but can be emotionally drained from their non-engaged colleagues.

▸ They exhibit *intentional* engagement.

Highly Engaged – Influential

These are your star players – your ambassadors – your go-to team members. They are always "All-In." These people will strive to build and maintain teams, constantly sharing messages that influence everyone. They attempt to unify the entire team and strive to transform those who are in the *non-engaged* category. Highly engaged people should be provided more time to speak at meetings, so they can model the desired behaviors and attitudes you wish to experience from the rest of the team.

> ▸ They exhibit *influential* engagement.

What level are your *engaged* people operating at? While we would like everyone to be engaged at the highest levels, I have discovered that the *Highly Engaged* – those who bring their A-game every day – represent only about 10% of the workplace. Let's put that into perspective for a moment. How would you feel if I told you that only 10% of the people serving in our military were highly engaged? What words come to mind? When I ask this question in my seminars and workshops people reply quickly with, "Scared," "Afraid," and "Nervous."

How long would our military be effective if only 10% of the two million men and women defending our freedoms were highly engaged? Think of the disastrous effects if 68% (1,360,000) of our Soldiers, Airmen, Sailors, and Marines were on the *non-engaged* side. Success would be impossible and that is precisely why each branch of the Armed Services ensures that their people speak a language that fosters success. They pick their side.

In the military, *non-engagement* is not an option and it is dealt with immediately when it arises. In the business sector, *non-engagement* is a constant option; a reality, so severe that it is almost expected. Why are we not scared, afraid, or nervous about it in the workplace? We should be. When *non-engagement* is enabled, yes enabled, we will eventually lose people – typically those on the *engaged* side.

Non-engagement is a choice that people make based on their perceptions of the environment and we already know that "perception is...", according to the popular saying, "reality." It does not say that perception is right or wrong, or even the truth. It states that it is a reality and people are highly influenced by their realities. This is why we need more highly engaged people – influential engagement.

Sound Bite:
Communication is the key to raising engagement because our phraseology influences perceptions.

When we allow low engagement levels in the workplace, we ride a fine line between a non-engaged environment and a hostile environment. As a business coach, I often go deep into the weeds with business leaders, uncovering problems, and discovering solutions. I have plenty of experience dealing with HR issues that can quickly escalate into something that could have a significant impact on the entire business and the team.

LANGUAGE - HOSTILE OR FRIENDLY?

According to the *Department of Defense Dictionary of Military and Associated Terms*, the words hostile and friendly are used to define those who are against you and those who are with you – those who oppose your mission and those who support it. While you and your team are not going into combat situations, a hostile environment in the workplace may often feel like a war zone. Hostile environments divide people. Friendly environments unify people.

I know that you may be thinking, "We do not have a hostile environment." You are probably right, but the lack of a unified language causes us to dangerously straddle the fence between hostile and friendly. So, let's take a look at the meaning of both words so we can make a better determination of the outcome of our spoken language. I underlined the keywords.

Hostile: of or relating to an <u>enemy</u>, marked by <u>malevolence</u>: having or showing <u>unfriendly</u> feelings, openly <u>opposed</u> or <u>resisting</u>, <u>not hospitable</u>, having an <u>intimidating</u>, <u>antagonistic</u>, or <u>offensive nature</u>.

Friendly: showing <u>kindly</u> interest and <u>goodwill</u>, serving a <u>beneficial</u> or <u>helpful</u> purpose, <u>favorably</u> disposed; inclined to <u>approve</u>, <u>help</u>, or <u>support</u>: <u>not hostile</u>.

Can a non-engaged environment become a hostile environment? Yes! With 68% of the workforce non-engaged, it's easy to see that most of our challenges and complaints come from that section of the team. Disengaged people are often those who eventually refer to an environment as hostile, which is only one step further than *miserable*.

According to Indeed.com, "A hostile work environment makes it challenging for employees to effectively do their job. For companies, this is an issue because a hostile work environment impacts both employee satisfaction and productivity." Keep in mind that the purpose of this chapter is not to provide training regarding harassment in the workplace, but to better understand the vital role that phraseology plays in the perception of a hostile environment. Below are ten common behaviors that could be interpreted as *hostile*. I took the liberty of underlining those involving a form of communication – either words or phrases.

Hostile Environment Behaviors

- Sexual activity discussion
- Physical comments
- Demeaning terms
- Inappropriate language
- Offensive jokes about sex, race, disability
- Sexually suggestive pictures
- Unneeded touching
- Rude gestures
- Work sabotage
- Threatening behavior

Half of these behaviors are directly related to communication – *words* and *speeches* (Parts I and II). The other half are directly related to our *gestures* and *actions* (Parts III and IV). To not take the impact of workplace language seriously can be a catastrophic mistake. The lackluster dialogue that occurs in most companies is the breeding ground for *non-engagement* and it also accounts for a significant number of instances that cause the business to be referred to as miserable or even *hostile.*

Like a hostile environment, non-engagement makes it challenging for people to effectively perform their duties, let alone to achieve the results needed to succeed. Non-engagement always impacts those who are engaged, affecting both team member satisfaction and customer satisfaction. A casual approach to choosing the right language will *divide* your people.

Which work environment do you feel leads to success – hostile or friendly? Like me, I think you would agree that we need to strive for a friendly environment. I am not saying that you need to be everyone's friend to foster a friendly environment, just as you do not need to be everyone's enemy to create a hostile environment. Our language either divides or unifies.

PHRASEOLOGY – DIVIDING OR UNIFYING?

According to Edmund De Waal, "With languages, you're at home anywhere." When business owners and leaders describe their company cultures to me, many refer to their people as a family, which is a noble aspiration. But I can quickly determine what type of family they have through the language spoken in their workplace. Some businesses claim to have a family feel but it is more of a *dysfunctional* family than a *directional* family. Dysfunctional teams feel detached – divided. Directional teams feel attached – unified.

 **Sound Bite:**
Dysfunctional business families lack an understanding of where they are going. Directional business families know their vision and destination.

When we think about improving the phraseology used in our workplace, most people immediately focus on what should not be spoken – removing foul language. It is common sense that profanity, like using the f-word, could do more than prohibit success – it can create a hostile environment. Offensive words and phrases should be removed. Some are easy to recognize but others are not. Yet, all *dividing phraseology* spoken makes a harmful impact.

If certain things should not be said in the workplace, because of the negative impact they make, then it suffices to say that certain things should be said to promote a positive and friendly work environment. Our ability to quickly identify phraseology as *unifying* or *dividing* is paramount to foster success at the highest levels.

Dividing Phraseology:

Everything we say matters, regardless of our audience or the topic. Everything we allow to be said matters, too. Whether we speak in a meeting, a one-on-one conversation, or a conference call over the phone or virtually, it is essential to exclude toxic or hostile comments which cause *dividing phraseology*. While most of us readily avoid the obvious choices that could be considered offensive, derogatory, or shameful, many inadvertently speak in ways that slowly divide the team.

Below is a list of the most common forms of *dividing phraseology* I have encountered in the workplace. These tend to be part of the current language and are spoken fluently... and unfortunately, too often. The list can go on and on but we must start to recognize divisive sayings and eliminate them from our vocabulary. I have added some of the possible interpretations after many of them.

- "It's not my job" – like nails on a chalkboard, this phrase, even if accurate, signals a lack of caring.
- "That's above my paygrade/I don't get paid enough for this" – understood to mean I don't earn enough money to care and usually said by a leader – imagine the impact.
- "It's not fair"
- "We don't have the bandwidth" – a polite way of saying "No."
- "Here's why it can't be done" – this comes across as "I give up."
- "I need a drink" – said to be funny but this quirky saying opens many interpretations about the person saying it.
- "That's not my problem"

- "I'm looking for a *warm body*" – announced by leaders desperate for someone to fill a position but it conveys a willingness to settle for the wrong team member.
- "I don't know" – the better way to say this is, "Let me find the answer."
- "It's not my fault" – I take zero responsibility.
- "There's nothing I can do."
- "I'll try" – I am probably going to fail.
- "I hate this company/these people" – usually mumbled under someone's breath but heard by everyone. This impacts the environment significantly.
- "But we've always done it this way" – I am incapable of or unwilling to learn something new and potentially better.
- "Here we go again" – I have absolutely zero faith in this working.
- "That's impossible" – let's not even try.
- "I don't care" – no explanation necessary but it speaks volumes.
- "I don't have time" – yes, there is always time for something that has value and will benefit the team.
- "I'm too busy" – remember, this is code for I am not engaged and sends the message that you are way too self-centered.
- "Whatever..." – I couldn't care less.
- "Um..." – each time this word is mixed into our speeches, it diminishes the meaning of our message and conveys that we lack belief in what we are saying. Remember, words are powerful.
- "Because I'm in charge" – undoubtedly, we all have flashbacks to our parents saying, "Because I'm the parent, that's why!"
- "I was just doing what I was told" – I follow orders but I am not responsible for the outcome or for common sense.
- "I quit" – only say this if you truly mean it because it sends a powerful message when you fail to follow through.

Sound Bite:
Failure becomes commonplace when the accepted phraseology in our workplace pushes people apart.

We must not only watch what we repeatedly say, because it becomes the accepted language in our environments, but we must listen to the way others speak to each other. The phraseology that does not serve the success of your team needs to be addressed and enhanced.

Borderline Phraseology:

Wait a minute! I know that you were expecting the next section to be on *Unifying Phraseology*, right? Is there a third type of phraseology? No, not really. These are the unique phrases that hover closely between unifying and dividing. I believe they are often said with good intentions but deliver bad results.

- "I'm a perfectionist" – plain and simple, stop using this one. Perfection is impossible, so you are clearly letting people know that you always fall short of your individual expectations. Do not attempt perfection, let your message be to strive for progress.
- "I need this yesterday" – an attempt to create a sense of urgency but absolutely impossible to achieve anything in the past, unless you can drive a DeLorean with a flux capacitor at 88 mph (*Back to the Future* reference).
- "Playing nice in the sandbox" – you have a professional workplace – a business – not a playground. This phrase implies that you perceive your co-workers as children. While some may act like that (because of the current language spoken), do not enable it further.
- "A man of few words" – I get it... you may attempt to speak *little* and say *much* but it can also convey that you have personal communication issues, you are unapproachable, and are easily bothered by others.

- "I'll just do it myself" – often said in frustration when someone else drops the ball but it conveys a lack of trust in your team and that you could be a control-freak.
- "No problem" – instead of saying, "you're welcome," which is the courteous and proper reply, this quick-phrase diminishes the person's appreciation and implies the person who received your help has been a bother and their objective could have been a problem.
- "This might be a stupid idea but..." – this immediately discounts the impact of what you are about to say and divulges the lack of value you place on yourself and your message. Instead, be confident when you share your insights, especially if they could unify others.
- "Let's give it 110%" – if we want people to trust us, we must be honest, and this phrase is a lie – it is physically impossible for your people to give anything more than 100%. When we ask them to, we already cause unwanted stress and anxiety. Instead, encourage your people to give it their best.

According to MarketWatch.com, if you've tried to influence your people by using any of these phrases, "they stopped listening to you long ago." According to a study by OnePoll and Jive Communications, 27% of your colleagues "tune out as soon as they hear you say them." Listen closely to your language and the language of others in your workplace because the *borderline* choice can jeopardize the unification of your team and the success of your business.

Unifying Phraseology:

It is time to grab your *Communication Bar* because we are about to raise it on the language you speak to further unify your people. But consider yourself warned. Any time you and your team actually "raise the bar," some people will step up and others will step out. But to use a cliché from earlier, whether people step up or they step out, "it's a win-win" for you, your team, your customers, and your business.

As with any new action, consistently using phraseology that fosters high levels of success will take practice. But I have found that the attractive and enticing feeling from an empowering language is contagious. As human beings, we communicate and our phraseology is critical for exceptional results.

Below are some of the unifying sayings that should be spoken as part of your language - regularly, confidently, and with your whole *heart* and *soul* poured into them. Always make sure the team understands the meaning of your message.

- "We need to all get on the same page" – when you say this, show your people the page... of the book you are jointly reading or the page of your Flight Plan (strategic plan), to get everyone focused on the Flight Levels (goals) required for <u>success</u>.
- "I appreciate you/I appreciate what you did" – showing appreciation far exceeds the impact of a mere "thank you." But do not hear what I did not say... "thank you" is highly important, too.
- "You made an impact" – never just give a high-five or an attaboy. Consistently share how your people made an impact and they will continue this behavior.
- "What you did was invaluable" – this is a great way to add value to the action your team member just took.
- "Failure is not an option" – it is if you do not identify what constitutes a failure. You must also address the steps for <u>success</u> and encourage your people to take them with urgency.
- "Lead by example" – use this often and back it up with examples. Speak the way you want others to; act the way you want others to. Think like a leader, act like a leader, speak like a leader.
- "I trust you" – a disengaged team lacks trust. Use this phrase often to build it back up.
- "That's a fantastic question" – this simple comment encourages everyone to ask better questions. Silence hinders <u>success</u>.
- "Thank you for speaking up in the meetings" – while encouraging your people to use *tact* while talking, I love this phrase because it permits your people to do more than attend meetings – they become active participants.

- "You made a tremendous difference" – lets people know that you value them and they are important to the results of your business, your team, and your clients.
- "Let's learn from our mistakes" – this reaffirms that you are not a perfectionist but rather an agent of progress. This also encourages people to take acceptable risks to guarantee success, rather than remain inactive and miss opportunities.
- "Don't change anything, enhance everything" – as your business grows, from all of the <u>success</u>, things will need to ~~change~~ (I mean enhance). This eliminates the fear, worry, and anxiety associated with *change.*
- "Stop selling – start sharing" – reinvigorate your sales team to unleash their true potential by eliminating the negative perceptions of typical salespeople.
- "Don't close deals; open opportunities" – this further empowers your sales team to avoid the awkwardness of trying to *close* people and inspires them to open powerful new relationships. After all, we are all in the *people* business.
- "We need to speak the same language" – this is 100% correct (not 110%). Our language will influence our people, empower them, encourage them, and allow them to become part of something special and great.

Phraseology issues are an epidemic in today's workplace, resulting in the lion's share of mistakes, misunderstandings, and frustrations. These challenges are so commonplace in businesses that they are typically viewed as a fact of life and most people cannot imagine improvements ever happening. You cannot fix this without raising your *Communication Bar* and transforming the phraseology used in your workplace.

Sound Bite:
If you do not raise the Communication Bar in your business, who will?

NEGOTIATING FOR SUCCESS

Phraseology has an emotional impact on those who say it and those who hear it. "May the Force be with you" speaks volumes to Star Wars fans just like "I'll be back" does with Arnold Schwarzenegger fans. While your business is not an actual movie, we all need to strive to be the action stars in our workplaces, speaking like true heroes.

Success is only achieved through the activity of our people. The right language encourages people to take the actions needed for success. So, we cannot underestimate its impact. Even the smallest additions to the language spoken in the workplace can have the biggest impact. Success is not guaranteed; it is achieved. We *negotiate* daily for success.

"The sweetest two words in any negotiation are actually, 'That's right,'" says former FBI hostage negotiator Chris Voss in his book, *Never Split the Difference*. "Before you convince them to see what you're trying to accomplish, you have to say the things to them that will get them to say, 'That's right.'" In business, we are in a constant state of negotiating for success, because we have *engaged* and *non-engaged* team members. The language spoken is paramount and we need to strive to get our people to think, "That's right" whenever unifying language is spoken in our environments.

The *Shared Language of Success* unifies our people, forming a "team" mindset. A dividing language pushes people apart, forming a "me" mindset. Regardless if we speak in a unifying tongue or a dividing one, the impact may first be seen in the reaction of our people – their body language.

The next way we communicate is through the *Gestures we Make.*

Communication Catalyst

Engagement Enhancer

Description: Identify engagement levels in your workplace and the language required to raise them.

Time of Exercise: 60 minutes

Purpose: To identify and increase the use of the *Unifying Phraseology* required to increase engagement levels throughout the team.

Resources: 3x5 cards, pens, white board, white board markers.

Presentation:

- Discuss the current engagement levels of your team – the percentage of engaged and non-engaged team members. Identify what side people are on!
- Give a 3x5 card and a pen to each participant.
- Ask participants to list the *Unifying Phraseology* choices they would like to see used more in the workplace to raise engagement levels.
- List all the choices on a white board.
- As a team, discuss each choice and what the true meaning of each statement is.
- Identify all the possible situations someone can use *Unifying Phraseology* to increase the engagement levels of the entire team.

Debrief: Provide consistent training to identify *Unifying Phraseology* and how to communicate it effectively to everyone.

Part III

The GESTURES We Make

Of all the things you wear, your expression is the most important.

~ Janet Lane

Part III

The GESTURES We Make

Every Gesture Makes an Impact.

Marine Corps boot camp began as you might expect – with an explosion of colorful metaphors and intense language, most of which I cannot repeat here. Our Drill Instructors had no shortage of talking points as they barked orders at the highest levels of volume. When we replied, we were instructed to "sound off" at ear-splitting loudness. Of course, we could not speak at the high levels they demanded, at first, so we were forced to repeat phrases like "Sir, yes, sir" at the top of our lungs, hundreds of times, until our voices began to crack.

Boot camp was a non-stop heightened level of extreme and thunderous sounds. But it wasn't all yelling and screaming during our entry phase into the Marine Corps. There were moments dedicated to communicating without words; times that were focused on the power of sending messages without speaking. To become a Marine would also require that we paid close attention to the *gestures we make*. This is an overlooked yet powerful element that should be focused on in the business sector, too.

In the military, worldwide, perhaps the most significant, widely used, and universally understood gesture is the hand salute. This method of communication exists in the United States Army, Navy, Air Force, Coast Guard, and Marine Corps. Each service member is taught how and when to properly salute people within all branches of service. They all speak the same language with this simple, yet powerful gesture – it is a unification tool among every branch of the Armed Services.

Although the origin of the hand salute is uncertain, some historians believe it evolved during the latter part of the Roman Empire's reign. Initially, in the early years of the American military, the gesture involved removing your hat (cover). Later, the hand salute was modified, and service members touched their cover with their properly-positioned fingers. This has remained the standard practice since then and was what I learned at eighteen years of age.

When the young recruits of my platoon were taught how to salute, we were not instructed to merely raise our arms and touch our covers. Because there was a meaning behind this motion, we were taught to bring our arms up with a swift and purposeful motion, bending at the elbow, placing our thumb firmly along our forefinger, and with all fingers extended, popping our salute into place. Once the salute was returned, we purposefully returned our arms to their original positions.

Sound Bite:
Even the smallest gestures have the power to make the biggest statements.

GESTURES ARE BACKED BY INTENTIONS

Saluting was not done at our convenience, nor merely when we felt like it. We also did not randomly salute people. We intentionally saluted specific people when appropriate, and each salute had a single meaning – to show respect. Below is a list of persons entitled to receive a military salute:

- The President of the United States (Commander-in-Chief)
- Commissioned officers and warrant officers
- Medal of Honor recipients
- Officers of friendly foreign countries

In addition to specific people, a salute is also rendered:

- To the United States National Anthem

- On ceremonial occasions - change of command and military parades
- To uncased National Colors outdoors
- When the Pledge of Allegiance to the U.S. flag is being recited outdoors
- At reveille, retreat, and taps – the raising or lowering of the flag
- During the sounding of honors

The salute always begins with the junior member saluting first. This gesture is required when service members are in uniform and they recognize those who are entitled (by rank) to receive a salute. So, let's think about the significance of the hand salute in the military culture. A salute is a form of showing respect and it is required, not optional.

In other words, respect is required in the military, among all members, and within all branches. It is one gesture, performed thousands of times each day and it has meaning. It communicates respect. What gestures are happening in your workplace? What message are they communicating? Are any of them increasing the respect level among your people? Are they having a positive impact or a negative impact?

 **Sound Bite:**
Gestures are happening in your workplace and ignoring them does not diminish their impact.

By no means am I suggesting that you update your Team Member Handbook to include a new policy on saluting. That will absolutely not work in the business sector. But imagine the possibilities if the gestures in your workplace communicated *respect*, or other positive feelings, by the members within each department and between the members of each department in your business. The possibilities are limitless, especially by eliminating silos and the dreaded "us vs. them" mindset.

Instead of implementing the hand salute at your next meeting, I highly suggest assessing the messages that are being sent to your people with the non-verbal communication happening currently in your workplace. Let's start by understanding the definition of *gesture* so we can identify the true impact of what happens when they occur in your environment.

gesture

noun

- a movement of part of the body, especially a hand or the head, to express an idea or meaning.
- the use of motions of the limbs or body as a means of expression.
- a movement usually of the body or limbs that expresses or emphasizes an idea, sentiment, or attitude.

So, by these definitions, a gesture is a movement; a motion that expresses meaning. Are the gestures used by your people expressing unification or division? We must not only be aware of our body language but constantly be on the lookout for the non-verbal communication used by our people that "speaks volumes" throughout our workplace. Every gesture is a critical motion in *The Communication Movement* happening in your environment right now.

MOTIONS SIGNIFICANTLY IMPACT MOMENTUM

I have never met an entrepreneur, business owner, or executive leader who answered "No" when I asked, "Do you want to achieve business momentum?" No one wants to see their business remain still, lacking the motion necessary to move toward their goals. But that is precisely what happens when the workplace is plagued with the wrong gestures. Poor body language will not only divide your team but it will cause your business to lose momentum, or worse yet, to move backward.

There is a huge difference between merely making progress and creating significant momentum in an organization. The phenomenon of business momentum is elusive to many because of the divisive gestures flowing throughout their workplace by their team members. Although business momentum is intangible, we can feel it when we have it – everything moves forward and upward, team members are proactive and positive, goals are set and accomplished, vision is shared and achieved, and customers are happy and referring your business to others.

Body language is not only a key indicator of attaining business momentum, but it is also an integral part of your culture. Without getting too deep into physics, *momentum* is a term used to describe *the quantity of* motion *of a moving body* - the greater the momentum, the harder it is to stop the object's movement. Let's directly translate the scientific description of momentum into a business equation so we can understand the power of motion created with our people.

1. Every *gesture* in the workplace is a *motion*.
2. *Motion* impacts our ability to achieve *business momentum*.
3. *Business momentum* is the quantity of *motion* of our peoples' bodies.
4. The greater the *business momentum*, the harder it is for our competition to stop us.

Unifying motions (gestures) lead to consistent levels of business momentum, which leads to increased motivation in our people, which leads to motivated people creating new opportunities and achieving greater results. *The Body Language Equation* is a simple formula to develop an unstoppable team, outpace your competition, and accomplish your mission.

> ## Motion + Momentum + Motivation
> ## =
> ## Mission Accomplishment

Do you have a Mission Statement? You should have one and talk about it often, so, when you say "Yes" to business momentum, you say "Yes" to ensure that the gestures in your workplaces are *Mighty* (unifying), not *Malevolent* (dividing).

MOTION DETECTORS

To protect our people from the negative (and dividing) consequences of destructive body language, we need to think of ourselves as Team Motion Detectors in the workplace. A real motion detector (or motion sensor) is the primary component of any security system. Its key purpose is to detect when someone is in your home when they shouldn't be there. In business, it is necessary to detect motions that could lead to danger – gestures in your workplace that shouldn't be. In the business sector, dangerous motions happen every day but people typically fail to address them, even though they are threatening the security of the workplace environment.

Sound Bite:
Like a home security system, detect the motions of your people, and remove the negative ones.

Could you imagine your home security system going off and just ignoring it? That makes no sense if you care about the people living in your home. It also makes no sense to ignore the signs of divisive gestures in your workplace environment – if you care about the people working there. To ensure that the motions (body language) of each Marine aligned with the mission of the Marine Corps, we were taught a specific leadership trait – bearing.

According to the Marines, "Bearing is defined as the way one conducts and carries him or herself in a manner that reflects alertness, competence, and control." As a Marine, I was expected to hold myself to the highest standards of personal conduct and to never be content with meeting only the minimum requirements. That went for the other two-hundred thousand Marines serving, as well.

As you can imagine, communication in the military is vital – life and death – so, every gesture is equally important because of the message it sends. The business workplace, while rarely a life-and-death scenario, must have a close watch on the signals, messages, and meanings sent from each gesture made by our people.

If you want to maximize the power of *The Body Language Equation*, it's time to identify and remove any *Malevolent Motions* and foster an environment of *Mighty Motions.* To ensure that our gestures send the right message, we are going to focus on the three elements of motion to further unify our people.

The Three Mighty Elements of our GESTURES:

1. Nonverbal Cues Reveal Clues
2. Body Language Shapes Trust
3. Physical Motions Foreshadow Action

Communication Catalyst

Four Up!

Description: Team members learn to communicate using nonverbal instructions.

Time of Exercise: 10 minutes (set up and exercise)

Purpose: To teach people how powerful their nonverbal communication is and how it has the power to move people.

Resources: A chair for each participant and a timer (stopwatch).

Presentation:

- Have all 5 people sit in their chairs, facing each other in a circle.
- Set the timer for 5 minutes.
- Have 4 participants stand.
- Start the timer and follow the rules:
    a. 4 participants must always be standing but no one can stay standing for more than 10 seconds.
    b. Using nonverbal commands only, participants instruct each other to either sit or stand.
    c. Keep going until one person stands for more than 10 seconds, less than four people are standing, or a verbal command is used.

Debrief: After the session, discuss ways to improve nonverbal communication in the workplace. This exercise is designed to increase teamwork through gestures and motions, allowing people to rely on each other without their voices.

Chapter 7

Nonverbal Cues Reveal Clues

The Visual Language we "Hear" with our Eyes.

My last day of service in the Marine Corps was Aug 23, 1991. I began my civilian life right after the first Gulf War ended and I started my filmmaking classes at Orange Coast College in Costa Mesa, California. Although I was using my G.I. Bill to help pay for school, I still needed to work to take care of my family. One of my first jobs was in the Electronics Department at K-Mart. I was excited to learn anything I could about the consumer side of the entertainment industry but instead of an education in home electronics, I received a valuable lesson in the power of body language.

I remember excitedly attending my first "Manager's Meeting," an all-company gathering with the entire store team. It sounded important to me, so I dressed up for it – slacks, a button-down shirt, and a tie. I quickly realized that I may have been the only one who felt this way, as no one else dressed up. While I cannot recall what the manager talked about that day, I vividly remember the body language of his team – it spoke volumes. Arms were crossed, there were plenty of eye rolls, heads were occasionally shaking, and some well-timed sighs happened to infiltrate his speech. I think some people may have even smuggled lemons into the meeting based on the sour looks on their faces.

This Manager's Meeting was certainly different than the All-Hands Meetings I had become accustomed to in the Marine Corps. Those meetings were always high energy, and everyone exuded enthusiasm and professionalism. The room was called to attention as the senior officer entered and every Marine immediately stood, remaining motionless at the position of attention. The commanding officer (CO) took the stage and with a confident "At ease," we sat back down and listened to his message.

When the CO said something motivating, his speech received a few unrehearsed "Ooh-Rahs," signaling excitement and agreement. There were no crossed arms, eye rolls, shaking heads, or sighs. The body language of each of the Marines sent a message of respect, pride in their identity, and commitment to the reputation of their beloved Corps.

At the Manager's Meeting, I was impacted by the body language of my co-workers, and I discovered immediately that the slightest gestures could, and often did, *move* everyone. In the business sector, the body language being used rarely translates into excitement and agreement. What impact is body language having on your team?

Sound Bite:
Body language says a lot about how people feel about respect, team identity, and the reputation of the business.

I have been in the business sector for over thirty years now and when it comes to body language in the workplace there is a missing element – *bearing*. There was a reason the Marines taught us this leadership trait within the first few days of boot camp. When bearing is absent everyone feels it. The body language I experienced at K-Mart conveyed the lack of interest, focus, and passion of the people present. To say that it was dismal was an understatement.

The intentional *gestures of division* were not an isolated incident as I soon discovered. In addition to working at K-Mart, I worked at a video rental store and grocery store, and lackluster body language was visible at both. Later, I worked at the film and video Equipment Center at the University of Southern California, then became the Vault Manager of Pacific Ocean Post. Unfortunately, negative body language existed at a private university and a high-end post-production facility, too.

It was also noticeable at the media company when I started as an entry-level scheduler. Before we could soar to over 300% growth, I needed to assess the body language in our environment and the messages that were silently being sent. As I worked my way to become the vice president, I discovered solutions to the divisive nonverbal cues happening.

DOES BODY LANGUAGE REALLY MATTER?

Understanding someone's intended message is not limited to the communication we *hear*; it is also experienced by the communication we *see*. Everyone wants success but not everyone studies the nonverbal cues that hinder the success they are striving for. I just typed *success* into Google and 2.5 billion results came back. That's a lot to sift through but not as many as the results that came back for *body language* – 4.7 billion.

Body language matters but most people do nothing to ensure that the nonverbal cues in their organization convey the right messages! Nonverbal communication is an essential element of the *Shared Language of Success* and it is happening right now, in your workplace environment. It encompasses a wide array of physicalized cues and depicts the emotional state of the communicator. To ignore body language in the workplace is a critical mistake made by too many leaders.

Different parts of the body help to deliver messages sent through nonverbal communication. Although some are subconscious on the part of the communicator, most are conscious choices to send a message using the body. Nonverbal communication is a part of life and most of it happens in your business with little or no attention paid to it. Some forms, like a handshake, a head nod, or a thumbs-up occur seamlessly in our interactions with others. They are unifying gestures and deliberately convey subtle messages that reveal the intent of the communicator.

We often pay very little attention to most nonverbal cues when they happen because they are not divisive in nature. However, if the middle finger shoots up at someone in the workplace, we will not only notice it and understand the message, but we will likely address this extremely offensive gesture and consequences will be enforced. Unfortunately, very little attention is given to the other subtle gestures that deliberately convey negative messages in the workplace, and virtually no consequences are issued, which further enables this destructive behavior.

Crossed arms, shaking heads, and eye rolls are only the tip of the iceberg regarding the nonverbal cues that reveal unhappy and disconnected team members at work. To grasp the true meaning of the message behind each body motion, we need to decode nonverbal communication and break it down into specific types, so we can increase the unifying gestures occurring in the workplace and transition out the dividing ones. While there are many forms, let's focus on the six main types.

6 Main Types of Nonverbal Communication:

Kinesics: body movements such as hand gestures and head movements are easily controllable and recognizable forms of nonverbal communication. Examples include a thumbs-up or a confident head shake.

Proxemics: how humans use space when communicating – the physical distance people put between themselves and others. This can be heavily influenced by a person's human culture, not just the workplace culture.

Posture: the position or bearing of the body – how we sit or stand communicates much about our attitude and emotional state.

Eye Contact: one of the primary ways that human beings express emotional information, either their interest or disinterest in a topic or situation.

Physical Touch: many interactions begin with an exchange of physical contact, like a hug or a handshake. A simple touch can send powerful messages and may easily be misinterpreted in the workplace.

Facial Expressions: often difficult to genuinely control, and perhaps the main indicator of someone's disposition and attitude, gestures like a frown or a smile immediately express the communicator's emotional state.

There are other ways to categorize nonverbal communication, such as physiology and paralanguage. According to the American Physiological Society, physiology is "the study of how the human body works under normal conditions. You use physiology when you exercise, read, breathe, eat, sleep, move, or do just about anything." Paralanguage, while it may include some gestures and facial expressions, typically addresses properties of speech such as tempo, vocal pitch, and manners of speaking.

I have left both of these descriptions out because they are too overarching, and we can readily use the six types mentioned above to capture and interpret the majority of gestures impacting the workplace environment. When it comes to the nonverbal cues happening in your business, be on the lookout for the subtle motions that can cause huge disconnections among members of your team.

SIGN LANGUAGE

For those unable to communicate with words and phrases (mute), or those unable to hear words and phrases (deaf), their primary means of communication is to *sign*. Figure 1, from NIDCD – National Institute on Deafness and Other Communication Disorders, shows the twenty-six specific signs known as the American Sign Language Alphabet, which allows people to communicate through Fingerspelling.

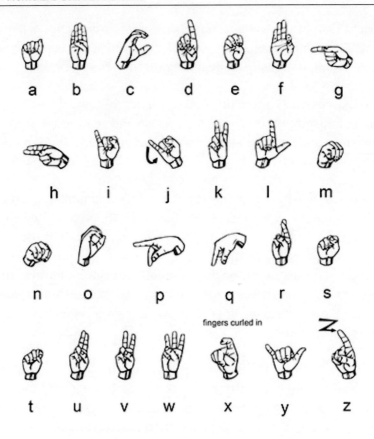

Figure 1 - American Sign Language Alphabet

There are also thousands of additional signs used to communicate through bodily movements. Every motion, hand gesture, body movement, and facial expression conveys meanings – not words. A single sign may express an entire sentence that would require three or more spoken words. To alter the meaning of a sign, one can simply shift the hand's orientation, the speed of the motion, or the angle of the movement. Part of the basics of sign language is being able to convey your feelings and emotions – as signs.

Sign language is a powerful example of the close relationship between how we think and how we gesture. Like sign language, most of the nonverbal cues in the workplace are directly linked to feelings and emotions, expressed not with words but with body language. Unfortunately, most of the signs used in the business sector do not unify people. Instead, they express divisive feelings and emotions.

Sound Bite:
Even the smallest gesture packs enough of a punch to completely knock out team engagement.

MILITARY HAND AND ARM SIGNALS

Sending a message with a hand salute was not the only gesture we learned in the military. Because many situations are life and death, and require complete silence, shouting commands is not a viable or wise option. Hand and arm signals are one of the most common forms of communication used by the military when "radio silence" is in effect and the troops need to remain undetected by the enemy.

Service members are taught to use specific hand and arm signals that allow for a wide range of actions to happen in complete silence. These nonverbal cues are heavily used by troops in the most challenging and dangerous situations. Below are some examples of the messages that can be communicated among the ranks with nonverbal cues.

- Disperse
- Increase speed
- Create a line formation
- Fix bayonets
- Map check
- Get a headcount
- Commence firing
- Rally
- Rush
- Air attack
- Take cover
- Take a knee
- Danger area
- Cease firing

This list only scratches the surface of the gestures that are paramount for mission accomplishment. We were also taught signals to let us know about a "Chemical, biological, radiological, or nuclear" attack. Figure 2, from US Army Training Circular (TC) 3-21.60 (Visual Signals), shows some of the hand signals used in the military for close-range engagements.

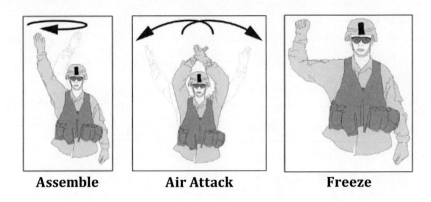

| **Assemble** | **Air Attack** | **Freeze** |

Figure 2 – Visual Signals, US Army

Not only do hand and arm signals instruct movement among the troops, but they are also used to control and guide mechanized units and vehicles, including aircraft. Can one gesture say so much? In the military, the answer is undeniably, "Yes." In your business, the answer is also undeniably "Yes." The difference is that the military trains its people to be fluent in speaking and fully comprehending body language. The business sector is often just aware that nonverbal cues are happening. They typically neglect to give body language the attention it deserves.

Hand signals have been used in many industries, especially in matters of safety. Police use hand signals to direct traffic. Workers on loading docks use hand signals to guide delivery vehicles. Gestures help crane operators, forklift drivers, and we even use them when riding bicycles to signal other vehicles of our intentions to turn left, turn right, or to stop.

Part of my training as a U.S. Marine included learning the basic infantry hand signals, like the ones mentioned earlier but as an air traffic controller, I was taught the additional hand and arm signals that were crucial on an airfield. These gestures, known as marshalling, directly translate to civilian aviation, too. Figure 3, from the International Air Transport Association's Ground Operations Manual, shows a few common examples of aircraft marshalling signals.

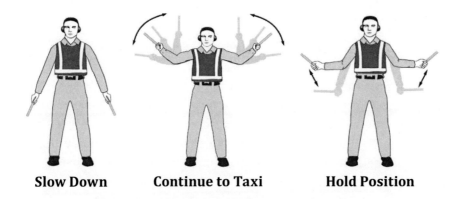

Slow Down   **Continue to Taxi**   **Hold Position**

Figure 3 – Marshalling Hand Signal for Aircraft

Marshalling is a form of visual communication that is an alternative to radio communication and is an integral part of aircraft movement on the ground. A Marshaller can typically be identified by their attire - reflective safety vest, helmet with acoustic earmuffs, and sometimes, their handheld illuminated beacons. Each movement is critical to passenger safety and spoken fluently by the marshallers and understood by the pilots.

There are roughly 50,000 flights per day with millions of hand and arm motions occurring to keep planes undamaged and passengers safe. Most passengers are not aware of the signals happening, and if they do see them, are unaware of their exact meaning. When we fly, it's okay to ignore the hand signals happening because the communication is intended for the pilot. In the business sector, nonverbal communication may be directed at one person but it impacts everyone.

Sound Bite:
There is too much at stake to remain unaware of the signals being sent through nonverbal communication.

BUSINESS BODY LANGUAGE

We have now seen examples of sign language, so people in the deaf/mute community can communicate. We have seen examples of the military arm and hand signals that allow large commands of troops to operate effectively in silence. We have also seen the importance of gestures when it comes to professions that have high regard for safety – law enforcement, construction, and aviation. In every single example, the highest level of dedication is given to each movement, motion, and gesture.

Every nonverbal cue reveals a clue about the intention, direction, and meaning of the communicator. Why is body language so critical in every example given but only mentioned in passing in the workplace? We do not attend training sessions on it, nor do we read about it in our "Employee" (Team Member) Handbooks. There are typically no policies and procedures to be found regarding body language to understand what is appropriate and what is not in the workplace. It is usually left to chance.

In most workplace environments, nonverbal cues are only discussed as a side effect of the negative impact they make – after the division has occurred. It is not uncommon to hear hallway mumblings like "I can't believe Sally rolled her eyes when Debbie was speaking" or "Did you see the way Dave was sitting in the meeting?" Unfortunately, these may be the extent of the body language discussions occurring in most businesses.

In the article, *What Body Language Experts Know That We Don't*, by Erin Van Der Meer, body language expert, Blanca Cobb states, "Reading body language is a bit like having a superpower. I see the subtle, nuanced elements of human communication." She has been called upon by the media to offer insights on everyone from celebrities and politicians to famous athletes and high-profile criminal cases. "The goal is always to understand people better," she adds.

With so much riding on the gestures made in the workplace, we must do a better job of deciphering the signals from our people. We need to acknowledge and make course-corrections before the nonverbal cues derail our culture. Like Cobb, our goal in business should be to better understand our people by paying closer attention to their nonverbal cues.

BODY LANGUAGE – BY THE NUMBERS

While most people focus heavily on what they say when they speak, in the end, the majority of our messages may be conveyed through our body language. But how much? When people discuss the studies of nonverbal communication, they tend to default to the following numbers – 7, 38, and 55. Professor Albert Mehrabian is known for his pioneering work in the field of nonverbal communication and his studies eluded to the fact that body language may be the major factor in understanding communication.

It was suggested that the person receiving the communication will focus on three factors to interpret communication – the words spoken, the tone of the voice, and the person's body language. The *7-38-55 Rule* implies that we trust the predominant form of communication, which happens to be body language. But let's see how each of the three factors rank in importance when understanding communication.

The 7-38-55 Rule

- Words   7%
- Tone of Voice   38%
- Body Language   55%

Since the release of his findings, and I am compressing the research he did in two studies (Mehrabian & Wiener, 1967 and Mehrabian & Ferris, 1967), people still refer to this rule as the gold standard and it is not uncommon to hear exaggerated claims that up to 90% of our understanding of communication is now nonverbal cues. So, is the 7-38-55 Rule accurate? Yes and No!

The findings were based on a specific context – when incongruent verbal and nonverbal messages meet at the same time. An example would be someone saying, "I'm fine" while shaking their head in anger and throwing their hands in the air. Their verbal communication is incongruent with their nonverbal communication. For decades, people have manipulated these findings to support their own narratives and Professor Mehrabian agrees!

Directly from his website, he states, "Please note that this and other equations regarding the relative importance of verbal and nonverbal messages were derived from experiments dealing with communications of feelings and attitudes (i.e., like-dislike). Unless a communicator is talking about their feelings or attitudes, these equations are not applicable."

While it is impossible to accurately determine an exact percentage that depicts the impact of body language in the interpretation of communication, it is undeniable that it is a force to be reckoned with – a force that conveys messages about our feelings and attitudes. Can one person, with a bad attitude, undermine an entire meeting? Absolutely, and we have all experienced it. One small gesture can have a significant impact on everyone.

NONVERBAL CUES REVEAL THE TRUTH

Jeremiah Andrew Denton Jr. (July 15, 1924 – March 28, 2014) retired from the United States Navy as a Rear admiral before becoming a U.S. Senator and representing Alabama from 1981 to 1987. On July 18, 1965, during the Vietnam War, he was piloting an A-6 Intruder while leading an air attack on a military installation. He was shot down and taken captive. As an American prisoner of war (POW) in North Vietnam, he endured seven years and seven months of horrific conditions, including solitary confinement and brutal abuse.

In 1966, he was forced to participate in a televised propaganda interview by his captors. The video of the broadcast finally made its way to the United States. He answered questions from a Japanese reporter under blinding television lights. While watching the interview, U.S. Naval Intelligence was able to decipher a message he sent, not with his words, but with his gestures.

As he spoke on camera, he answered questions about his views on the actions of the U.S. Government. In defiance of his captors, he reaffirmed his government's position, knowing that he would be punished. But it was his eyes that did the real talking – he blinked his message in Morse code. The word he blinked was heard loud and clear: "T-O-R-T-U-R-E."

Jeremiah Denton was released on February 12, 1973, during Operation Homecoming. He speculated that the North Vietnamese did not realize the blinking message he sent until 1974. The taped interview is now stored at the Records of the Central Intelligence Agency, among the holdings of the Special Media Archives.

Sound Bite:
Nonverbal cues can happen quickly and send deep messages – blink and you may miss them.

SEEING THE MESSAGES IN YOUR BUSINESS

The impact of body language is undeniable. But the focus on harnessing its power in the business sector is unacceptable. We can no longer "turn a blind eye" to the nonverbal cues in the workplace. They are integral forms of communication, not merely afterthoughts. Just like words and speeches, they move people. In my experience, they may move us with greater force than anything we say.

Never dismiss the nonverbal power currently flowing through your organization. It impacts everyone on your team and every one of your customers. As you may have guessed, the nonverbal cues in our organizations come in two categories, *unifying* and *dividing*. They convey a significant amount of information without anyone opening their mouths.

When our body language is unifying it sends messages of engagement, enthusiasm, and sincere interest. When body language is dividing it displays feelings of disconnection, apathy, and loathing. Every gesture not only sends a message but it is an important part of *The COMMUNICATION Movement* happening in your organization right now.

Remember the cliché "seeing is believing"? What messages are you sending with your body language? What messages are your team members sending with theirs? Reading body language may not be an exact science but it is critical to use our eyes to read the messages being sent in our environments.

Communication Catalyst

Find the Gestures

Description: Each team member lists as many gestures being used in the workplace – good and bad.

Time of Exercise: 60 minutes

Purpose: To identify the current gestures used by your team and the meaning behind each one.

Resources: 3x5 cards, pens, white board, white board markers.

Presentation:

- Give a 3x5 card and a pen to each participant.
- Ask participants to list as many gestures as possible that they have noticed in the workplace.
- Go around and have each participant share their list of gestures – list each one on the whiteboard.
- One at a time, pick a gesture and discuss the possible meanings that it can convey.
- Identify the gestures that would have a positive impact on people and those that would have a negative impact.

Debrief: Provide additional training sessions that include a discussion of the appropriate and inappropriate gestures allowed, and not allowed, in your workplace.

Chapter 8

Body Language Shapes Trust

Seeing is Understanding.

"I'm okay – I'm fine," she said to me. Those were Gina's exact words when I would ask how she was doing during her battles with cancer over the years. I asked her when she was diagnosed with non-Hodgkin's lymphoma, ten months after we were married. Later, I inquired as the chemotherapy coursed through her body, and as the high-energy waves of radiation attempted to kill her cancer cells. I asked her when she was recovering from breast cancer. I also asked her when she was coming back home after suffering from cardiac arrest.

No matter how strong she tried to be, and no matter what she said, I learned to read Gina's body language to decipher her true feelings – physically and emotionally. Sometimes, the words she spoke with her mouth did not align with what she was saying with her body. Everything from her eyebrows to the positioning of her feet could send messages to me. To be the best caregiver possible, I needed to be observant and be able to read the meaning of each signal.

Body language is critical in every marriage, but in ours, it has become a powerful way for me to gauge the real emotions being expressed by my wife, especially during her most challenging circumstances. I fine-tuned my fluency of body language during non-Hodgkin's lymphoma, basal cell cancer, breast cancer, melanoma, and cardiac arrest. Observing her communication, understanding it, and properly reacting to it has built the highest levels of trust between us.

Gina often did not want to let our young daughter know just how bad she was feeling. When Erika would ask, "Mommy, how are you feeling?", Gina's verbal response of "I'm doing good honey," was not as powerful as the glance she gave me, or the squeeze on my hand to let me know how horrible she was truly feeling.

Over the past twenty years of health issues, we have learned to rely on each other, sometimes deeply communicating volumes with a single look or motion. Trust is essential for every relationship we have – personally and professionally. It is critical for friendships to thrive, to be effective parents, and to have a successful marriage.

According to the American Psychological Association, up to 50 percent of marriages end in divorce. Think about that for a moment. 100 percent of those marriages began by taking vows – with their words. Is it possible that there was a trust issue in the relationship? Yes! A lack of trust is often cited as a major cause of divorce.

According to DivorceMagazine.com, "When thinking of reasons for divorce, many of us often think of infidelity, growing apart, and arguments over money matters as the main culprit. But the truth is, trust plays a large part in how successful your marriage will be. A marriage that lacks trust is surely headed down the road to divorce."

Sound Bite:
Body language signals the trust levels in your organization – pay attention to them.

LOOK FOR THE SIGNS OF TRUST

In the corporate world, trust is paramount for great results. According to the Harvard Business Review, "As a leader, you want people in your organization to trust you. We often see that trust is a leading indicator of whether others evaluate them positively or negatively." Their study shared data from 360 assessments of 87,000 leaders and they "looked for correlations in trust" and one of the key elements they discovered was "consistency."

Because trust is intangible and incredibly subjective, it may often be tough to define. But we can feel it when we have it and we can certainly experience it when it is lacking. Trust must be earned, and our body language shapes the levels of trust experienced by everyone seeing our gestures. Is the body language in your organization consistently building trust or unintentionally destroying it? Let's take a look at the definition of trust so we can identify the body language needed to support the levels of trust we desire in the workplace.

trust

noun/verb

- assured reliance on the character, ability, or truth of someone.
- to place confidence in; rely on; hope.
- to say or do something without fear or misgiving.

Based on these definitions, our body language speaks volumes about our character. It also allows people to believe in us, have confidence in us, and provides hope, encouraging people to trust in us without fear. We often hear how important it is to align our words and our actions. While I agree, we also need to focus our attention on the correlation between our words and our body language because each movement announces our true intentions and either strengthens or weakens trust.

Sound Bite:
Every time we speak with body language, we either raise or lower trust levels in our people.

Trust played a vital role when I served in the Marine Corps. As an air traffic controller, the trust between aviators and controllers was essential, not just for mission accomplishment, but also for safety. In the business sector, trust was monumental as I developed a team of leaders and we grew the media company to over 300% annual sales growth. As a financial services sales representative, trust was a key factor to allow my clients to share their personal financial information with me.

As a business coach, I know that trust is vital for me to deliver great results for my clients. I encourage business leaders to share data about their revenue and margins, their challenges and issues, their sales projections, and the behaviors of their people. If I cannot establish trust, I fail to receive the critical information I need to diagnose their business and make relevant solutions for improvements.

LEVELS OF TRUST

The success of every organization is directly linked to the body language "spoken" in their environments. While most people *talk* a good game, it is their body language that often *announces* the level of trust they operate at. I have discovered five levels of workplace trust. Can you identify the level of trust in your workplace, based on the body language of the people? Our goal is to work our way to the top – Level 1.

The 5 Levels of Trust in the Workplace

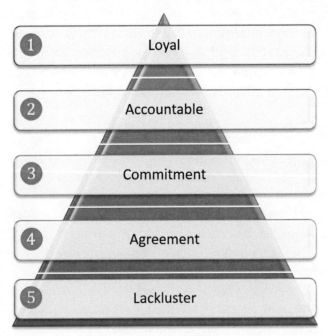

1. Loyal
2. Accountable
3. Commitment
4. Agreement
5. Lackluster

Trust levels, while rarely spoken about, are often best revealed through the behaviors of our people. Link the current behaviors of your team members with the behaviors detailed in each of the five levels. Check the boxes that apply.

LEVEL 1 - LOYAL
- ☐ Goes above and beyond for other team members.
- ☐ High levels of respect are displayed in and out of the organization.
- ☐ Focuses on making enhancements to the organization.

LEVEL 2 - ACCOUNTABLE
- ☐ Takes responsibility for issues and problems – finds solutions.
- ☐ Has an ownership mindset.
- ☐ High value is placed on accomplishing corporate goals.

LEVEL 3 – COMMITMENT
- ☐ Belief in identity – mission, vision, core values.
- ☐ Dedicated to the highest levels of excellence.
- ☐ Ensures that communication is crystal clear.

LEVEL 4 – AGREEMENT
- ☐ People only do what needs to be done – the bare minimums.
- ☐ Following policies and procedures.
- ☐ Satisfactory work levels – understanding of job expectations.

LEVEL 5 – LACKLUSTER
- ☐ Silos exist – us vs. them mentality.
- ☐ Complaining and finger-pointing – the blame game.
- ☐ Negativity, gossip, and rumors – derogatory discussions.

People may say they are loyal but their body language could reveal a lackluster trust level – a significant gap in the levels of trust, which can severely impact performance and results. Just as clay is transformed by the slightest amount of pressure in the hands of a master potter, every gesture, motion, and movement can alter trust in the workplace.

Sound Bite:
Body language is a clear indicator of the trust levels in our business – if we look for them.

BODY LANGUAGE IMPACTS CREDIBILITY

"You do solemnly state that the testimony you may give in the case now pending before this court shall be the truth, the whole truth, and nothing but the truth, so help you, God?" "I do." Hopefully, you have never had to take this oath in a court of law. But you are likely familiar with it. While everyone who takes the stand in a courtroom is under oath to speak the truth, most juries understand that many people still lie.

Testifying in front of a jury is said to be one of the most stressful situations we can experience, especially if you are the defendant accused of a crime, or the victim detailing the incident. The search for the truth may take months of back and forth banter between the prosecutors and defense lawyers, and everyone is under tremendous scrutiny.

Regardless of the words spoken from the stand, body language often helps to establish trust during a trial and allows juries to make a better determination of guilt or innocence. Any nervous gestures can cause the jurors to discount the witnesses' credibility, severely altering the case. In many cases, body language may inadvertently "testify" against a witness.

While we are not under interrogation in the workplace, it can often feel like it, especially if we are not aware of our body language. Credibility is critical for leaders and it could impact our potential to achieve peak performance from our people. For team members, credibility impacts their ability to work cohesively with one another and it is also necessary as we communicate to those outside of our team – customers, clients, vendors, etc.

Is body language building credibility or tearing it down with your people? Do their movements align with their words? There is much riding on everything we say and do, and body language constantly reaffirms our credibility. Just like in the courtroom, we are judged on our body language and each motion makes a significant impact on the level of trust we attain.

There is much at stake as we deliver nonverbal messages in the workplace. We cannot afford to have a disconnect between our voices and our body language but most people are completely unaware of the wide array of nonverbal faux pas they display each day. Whether we are aware or unaware, our body language moves people – either closer together or farther apart.

Sound Bite:
Body language either unifies (builds trust) or divides (destroys trust).

DIVIDING BODY LANGUAGE

Raising your hand is a gesture that implies you have a pending question. But if you are at an auction, that gesture announces that you are making a bid. There is the old myth that a man scratched his ear at an auction and inadvertently bought a painting for over $1,000,000. Fortunately, most auctioneers understand the difference between an ear scratch and a bid. In the workplace, we may not be so lucky.

Dividing body language is often referred to as negative or defensive body language, signaling that people are closed-off, detached, disinterested, upset, or unapproachable. While very few people show up to work to intentionally divide people with their gestures, some people in the workplace have this impact without even noticing.

Below are some of the most common examples of *Dividing Body Language* that shape the trust levels we experience in the workplace.

Clock Watching – Those who check the time regularly, especially in meetings, display a complete lack of value in the content being discussed and a total disregard for the people in attendance.

Phone Checking – When people constantly flip over their phones, checking to see if their next "critically important" call or message has come through, they appear disinterested in what is happening at the moment.

Fidgeting – Innocently moving about restlessly or playing with bracelets, pencils, or other objects may convey nervousness and boredom.

Poor Posture – When someone slouches, droops their neck and shoulders, or hunches forward, their body language can be interpreted as a lack of confidence and low self-esteem.

Avoiding Eye Contact – This always leaves a bad impression and may indicate a lack of trustworthiness. It can also be viewed as unprofessional.

Strong Eye Contact – People may feel that the person doing this movement is trying to be in control or even intimidate them when it is overly intense or for long periods.

Nail Biting – Not only a bad habit, and done without usually realizing it, nail-biting expresses stress, anxiety, or insecurity.

Nose Touching – When someone rubs or touches their nose, they may come across as being untruthful. It can also give a signal of disbelief or rejection.

Crossing Your Arms – Perhaps the most common *dividing* gesture, this conveys a defensive posture – a protective shield someone puts up as a barrier. It sends the message of being closed-off or closed-minded.

Fig Leaf Pose – Yes, this one references Adam and Eve. When a person stands with their hands in front of their groin area, it displays that they are uneasy or introverted. It may also indicate that the person feels unimportant – low self-esteem.

Steepling – This classic gesture is done to convey power by the person placing their fingertips together – in a steeple position. It subtly demonstrates that they feel like they are in charge.

The Eye Roll – Originally a form of flirting, this body gesture now conveys a different message – annoyance. It can show disagreement and is perceived as rude and unprofessional.

Tapping Your Feet – When people tap their feet and fingers or twirl their hair, they display anxiety and uncomfortableness.

Hands on the Cheek – When this happens, it not only indicates a person who is deep in thought but may also express that the person is disconnected from the conversation, preoccupied, or lost in other thoughts.

Head in the Hands – When someone hides their face in their hands they demonstrate being upset, ashamed, or are experiencing extreme boredom.

Hands in the Pockets – Sure, some people may do it because it feels comfortable but in a professional setting it suggests that the person is insecure and lacks confidence. This was a huge no-no in the Corps!

Body language habits come in all forms and can be hard to break. When they are *dividing* movements, they will significantly impact trust levels in the workplace, especially if they are constantly allowed. They will not merely go away on their own. People must be taught the impact of the language they speak with their bodies. Failing to address negative body language is not a solid strategy if you want to build trust.

Sound Bite:
Fixing bad body language begins by creating an awareness of the dividing messages being sent.

UNIFYING BODY LANGUAGE

In boot camp, we often operated on little sleep. When we sat down in a classroom to study our weapons, Marine Corps history, or rank structure, it was not uncommon for us to begin to doze off. Falling asleep in class sent a powerful negative message to our Drill Instructors and they reacted as you might imagine – loud and angry.

Instead of dozing off, we would slap the back of our own necks when we felt tired. The slight sting of each slap caused us to stay awake and was less painful than the punishment from our Drill Instructors if we fell asleep. I am not suggesting that slapping the back of your neck would be considered a unifying gesture in the workplace. In boot camp, however, it was an acceptable movement that sent a message of remaining alert during the classroom instruction.

What would be considered acceptable body language in your environment? What would unify your people? Let's take a closer look at some of the body language that can be added to your choices of nonverbal communication, to shape trust.

Below are some of the most common examples of *Unifying Body Language* that shape the trust levels we experience in the workplace.

A Firm Handshake – The keyword is firm, not painful. A solid handshake communicates respect and positive self-worth. Also, the person reaching out for the handshake first sends a message of confidence and professionalism.

Lean In – This subtle shift in the positioning of our body sends a powerful message that we are interested, in tune, and can be trusted. Just do not invade someone else's personal space.

Head Tilted – A slight tilt of the head to one side suggests that a person is listening intently and highly interested in what is being said.

Direct Eye Contact – You can easily show respect and confidence by looking at someone directly in the eye when speaking to them. A steady gaze, not overly gazing, sends a strong message.

Standing Straight – This stance, especially with our shoulders back, lets everyone know that you feel confident in yourself. Strive to be relaxed, not too rigid.

Stroking the Chin or Beard – The classic movement communicates being in deep thought and indicates high levels of interest in the discussion.

Rapidly Rubbing Hands Together – This quick movement can communicate that you are anxiously and excitedly awaiting something.

Head Nodding – This simple gesture speaks volumes, showing that you are listening and in agreement (a level of trust). When someone nods to acknowledge valid points or questions, everyone takes notice.

Stable Head – Many people tend to move their heads too much during conversations, signaling that they are distracted or uninterested. Maintain very little head movement to convey a huge message of being sincerely interested in the other person.

Hold Your Head Up – Refrain from looking down or away from the person you are speaking with and you will express confidence and genuine interest. Lowering your head or looking away could be interpreted as though you are hiding something.

Furrowed Brow – Your forehead – that space right above your eyes – is a billboard of signals. By raising your eyebrows, you may show surprise and questioning. By pulling it together, you can display sympathy and concern.

Touching – When following the common rules of etiquette, you may convey a personal connection – a deeper understanding. Light touching can display sympathy but can also be easily misinterpreted. Be cautious when using touch to send messages.

Smile – This simple and warm facial expression is often underutilized in the workplace. It can quickly convey happiness, hope, and positivity. Everyone should smile more!

Unifying body language, like everything else, requires balance. You are not expected to do all of these at the same time or simply use them as mere "checkbox" items. Rather, start with an awareness of the gestures that you and your team are making to ensure that the motion matches the intended message.

Body language sends the most accurate messages when delivered genuinely and sincerely. It opens the opportunity to build trust when it is non-aggressive, comfortable, and confident. When it comes to body language that shapes trust in the workplace, we must strive to remove the barriers between our people. Do not let dividing body language continue to hold back the unlimited potential of your team.

Communication Catalyst

Trust Builders

Description: Each team member lists ways the organization can be greater.

Time of Exercise: 60 minutes

Purpose: To work together toward new levels of greatness.

Resources: 3x5 cards, pens, white board, white board markers.

Presentation:

- Ask each participant if your organization can be greater. The answers should all be "yes."
- Give a 3x5 card and a pen to each participant.
- Ask participants "how" the organization can be greater.
- Pick one way the company can be better and have each person present ideas about the actions that can be taken to achieve those results.
- Write down all the steps required to achieve the level of greatness identified.
- Have an open discussion, to map out all the details to transform each idea into a reality, including timeframes, resources needed, and people required.

Debrief: Create a plan for each way the organization can be greater.

Continue to regroup with the team to discuss the steps taken, building trust along the way as enhancements are made to ensure success.

Chapter 9

Physical Motions Foreshadow Actions

Seeing What's About to Happen.

How would you like to be able to see what happens in the future? Would it be beneficial to be able to predict the patterns and behaviors of your people? To know what is coming, and not guess about it, would be a powerful tool for anyone who wants to accomplish goals, hit their mission, and achieve their vision (for the future). To anticipate with accuracy, the actions about to happen from your people does not require *precognition* – the psychic ability to see events in the future. You do not need to polish the crystal ball, shuffle a deck of tarot cards, or even cast magic spells.

When I coach business leaders, most struggle to guess how their teams will react to situations like the rollout of a new software program, updated policies and procedures, or shifts in the workflow. When referring to a lackluster reaction by their people, I cannot tell you how many times a leader has said, "I didn't see that coming." What if you can? Imagine knowing what to expect – from their actions. Learning to predict the actions of your people is much like forecasting the weather – *physical motions foreshadow actions*.

fore · sha · dow

verb

- to be a warning or indication of a future event.
- to represent, indicate or typify beforehand.
- to be a sign or give a hint before something happens.

Every day, our people give off warning signs – indications, and hints of how they will soon perform. Actions impact results, yet most leaders ignore the blatant nonverbal signs happening every day in the workplace. Would you ignore a weather forecast if it predicted a hurricane or a tornado? Highly unlikely. Just think about how many times you have checked the weather forecast, either by watching it on television or listening to it on the radio. We are all familiar with common weather signs, like the ones below, as indicators of what Mother Nature has in store.

Common Weather Signs

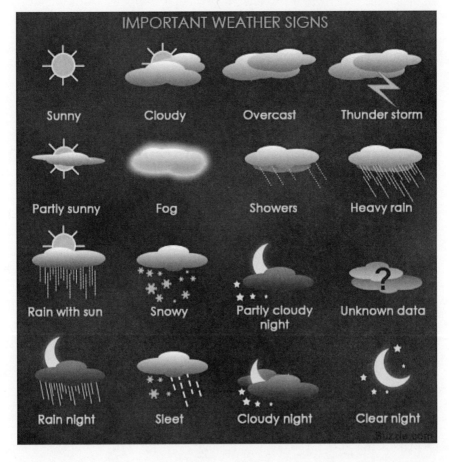

According to Sciencedaily.com, "Weather forecasts are made by collecting as much data as possible about the current state of the atmosphere (particularly the temperature, humidity, and wind) and using an understanding of atmospheric processes (through meteorology) to determine how the atmosphere evolves in the future." Simply stated, meteorologists look at the motions in nature to understand its future performance. In business, we often fail to look at the motions of our people to understand their future performance.

The physical motions of current weather conditions allow us to forecast rain, snow, tornadoes, hurricanes, high wind advisories, flash floods, and tropical storms. The purpose of forecasting is simple – to be better prepared to handle nature's future actions. To ignore a severe weather warning makes no sense. To ignore the business predictions available, by observing our people, makes no sense either.

How accurate can weather forecasts actually be? The weather website, SciJinks.gov, states that "A five-day forecast can accurately predict the weather approximately 90 percent of the time." Like a short-term weather forecast, the physical motions of your team allow you to accurately predict the behaviors they could exhibit soon.

Sound Bite:
Closely observe the current physical motions of your team to better predict their actions.

Growing up in Southern California, before cable television, we had very few television stations to choose from. I remember watching KABC, Channel 7, and their meteorologist Dallas Raines. There was very little inclement weather in Chino but occasionally, we had an exciting forecast about the possibility of rain, and sometimes it did get cold. I remember it hitting 50 degrees – whew! How did we survive in California? While it was difficult to be in such "cold" weather with shorts and flip flops, somehow, we endured.

When I was eighteen, I began to pay much closer attention to weather forecasts. In 1988, I was stationed at Marine Corps Air Station, Yuma Arizona, as an air traffic controller. Weather can significantly affect aircraft operations, so each pilot carefully calculated weather factors into their flight plans.

Forecasting weather conditions is such a critical aspect of flying that the Aviation Weather Center website runs 24/7, 365 days per year to provide vital information to pilots. Their mission statement is "The Aviation Weather Center delivers consistent, timely, and accurate weather information for the world airspace system. We are a team of highly skilled people dedicated to working with customers and partners to enhance safe and efficient flight."

WEATHER FORECASTS HELP US TO PREPARE

Yuma had no shortage of extreme heat. It was not uncommon to see the temperature rise to 120 degrees on a summer day. In addition to the scorching Yuma desert, I have also experienced extreme cold environments. Moving my family to Minnesota, in 2011, I quickly discovered that watching the weather forecast was a necessity. The range in temperatures throughout the year was significant. Minnesota could be as high as 90° degrees in the summer and as cold as -25° (without the windchill) in the winter. That is a 115-degree range.

Weather forecasts are important because they help us to predict future climate expectations and allow us to be better prepared for what's coming.

Weather Forecasts allow us to:

1. Prepare how we dress (for warm or cold weather, for rain, for snow).
2. Guide us to use additional gear (umbrellas, snow jackets, sunscreen).
3. Determine equipment usage (power cables, lights, speakers).
4. Plan outdoor activities appropriately.
5. Utilize proper vehicles.
6. Protect people with health issues (allergies, asthma).
7. Schedule work shifts.

Closely observing the actions coming from Mother Nature is a necessity when you live in regions with extreme weather. To ignore hazardous weather conditions could be dangerous, perhaps even fatal.

Closely observing the actions coming from your people is also a necessity when shooting for high levels of success. Ignoring the physical motions of your team could be hazardous to your business and your team.

Sound Bite:
Failing to forecast the upcoming actions of your people could send you directly into a storm you did not plan for.

Meteorologists strive to predict the upcoming behaviors of Mother Nature through *weather forecasts*. While forecasts are not always accurate, we still tune-in so we have a better idea of how to map out our day, know what to wear, and to anticipate traffic conditions. In the business sector, many people fail to observe the physical motions happening in their work environments. If we cannot tune-in to the *action forecast* in the office, we cannot predict the upcoming behaviors of our teammates.

WHAT'S THE FORECAST FOR ACTION?

Fortunately, we no longer need to wait for the evening news to know the weather forecast for tomorrow. With the swipe of a finger, we can easily check the five-day forecast on our phone apps. Think about how many times you have checked the weather in the last week. Now, think about how many times you have checked the physical motions of your team to determine their upcoming actions.

Most people spend more time listening to their local weather forecast than they do focusing on the *action forecast* of their people. Let's be clear about an undeniable fact - at the end of each day, our results will be achieved through the *actions* taken – by us and our people.

Action forecasts, in the workplace, are important because they help us to predict future expectations from our people and allow us to be better prepared for what's coming.

Action Forecasts allow us to:

1. Anticipate our team's focus on new goals.
2. Predict upcoming team morale.
3. Understand how people will embrace new technologies.
4. See how people will welcome new leadership/new team members.
5. Understand how people will react to new products and services.
6. Predict how people will accept updated policies and procedures.
7. Anticipate how our team will support the organization's plan.

In most businesses, leaders are often left disappointed by the actions, or inactions, of their people. When we fail to read the signs, we fail to be able to react. Everyone wants high levels of morale, a sense of urgency, and initiative to run throughout their workplace. That would be a positive forecast. Instead, many leaders are left with storms, tornadoes, and hurricanes of negative energy when they fail to observe the physical motions that were signaling foreshadowed actions.

What's the forecast like in your office? How does it feel when you speak to your people, or when they communicate with each other? Every day, our people are giving off data, through their physical motions that give us a momentary glimpse into their future actions. By now, you are probably ready to learn how to forecast the actions of your people, which either lead to success or failure.

Weather forecasts may be critical for industries like aviation, maritime, agriculture, forestry, utilities, and the military. But *action forecasts* are critical for every industry – for every business.

READ THE PLAY IF YOU WANT TO MOVE FORWARD

Do you want to win in business? I know that's an odd question. Of course, you do, especially if you are reading this book. In sports, all winning teams must learn to "read the plays" so they can anticipate the next move. In business, just as in sports, every move our team members make shows the next actions they are likely to take. Just observe the physical motions happening in your next meeting – they foretell the actions to follow or the inactions to foresee.

I played a lot of sports as a kid and it didn't matter if it was baseball or soccer, my coaches not only taught us to take action but how to anticipate it. In business, too many leaders focus only on teaching their people to do their job, but they rarely read their physical motions to ensure that their future actions will match the desired results.

In sports, physical motions foreshadow the actions coming. Players attempt to read the play, so they know which moves to make themselves. With millions at stake, most athletes strive to read the plays about to happen.

Football plays are designed to help the team to move forward – to score – to win. They are not intended to be easily read by the defense. When the competition knows your next move, you can easily lose yardage. Championship players, like quarterback Peyton Manning, could read the defensive alignment so well that he would often change the play with an audible before the snap of the ball. The defenses' physical motions influenced his actions. He understood the *action forecast*.

In a spread formation, when three or more receivers line up, it is an indicator that a passing play is about to happen. When extra blockers surround the ball, it announces a possible quarterback sneak or a run to gain short yardage. Players also make moves to fake out the competition by signaling a blitz when they actually intend to drop back to their original coverage positions.

The defensive line will study the running back's eyes just before a snap. The quarterback's body is closely watched to see which direction he will throw the ball. The wide receiver's motions suggest when he will take off. The line-up of the offense suggests the next play. For a defensive lineman to be successful it is not just about his speed or size, it's about his ability to see what's coming - to read the play quickly and react fast. Speed and size matter little if he fails to see what could be coming.

During any baseball game, most communication occurs between the pitcher and the catcher – with hand signals. The catcher can suggest, with either one, two, or three fingers, that the pitcher throws either a fastball, curveball, or a slider. By adding a fourth finger and a slight wiggle, he just requested a changeup.

A pitcher must read the runner, or he will steal a base. When a runner reaches a base, it gets more entertaining to watch the physical motions of the third-base coach. He may rub his belly to indicate a bunt, touch his ear to signal a base steal, or he may simply indicate a hit and run by lightly touching his nose. The third-base coach sends the signals for future actions by his current physical motions. Ignoring the *action forecast* could cost the game.

Volleyball players learn how to read their opponents. They increase the odds of getting a block by observing physical motions from the hitter. Paying attention to shoulder movement gives a good idea of the direction of the intended spike. Volleyball players also pay close attention to the hitter's eyes to determine the direction the ball will be going (the future action). But great hitters understand that their body language is being read, to predict their actions, so many players attempt to send a signal that is opposite of their intent.

Boxers and mixed martial arts fighters also study the physical motions of their opponents. By reading their body language correctly, they could knock them out, but reading it incorrectly could get them knocked out. Fighters know that where the eyes look, the attack will follow. When the arms are chambered, it signals an upcoming hand attack. When a back leg stiffens up, it may alert the other fighter to an impending kick. To survive the round, fighters also study the positioning of their opponent's torso and their breathing.

Sound Bite:
Understanding the motions of our people allows us to be proactive with our actions.

It's fair to say that you want to win, and you do not want to get knocked out in business. So, reading your peoples' physical motions is paramount. Like an offensive line taking the field, I could often read the plays of my sales team at the media company, as soon as I stepped into the office. Walking through the facility, I observed the body language of my entire team – looking for the physical motions that foreshadowed the upcoming actions or inactions.

Now, as a speaker, I read the room before I speak, and I constantly observe the room during my presentations. Are they leaning in or dozing off? Are they taking notes or checking their phones? Are they smiling and nodding, or are they frowning and crossing their arms? It makes a huge difference when my audience is interactive versus being silent. If I do not read the room correctly, it could impact my desired results.

As a business coach, I never sit down in the conference room without observing the physical motions of my clients and their teams. I am never hired so they can achieve worse results. I am only brought in to unleash the power of their leaders and their teams – to foster the actions that lead to greater results. If I overlook the physical motions of my clients' people, I miss the ability to understand the *action forecast* available to me.

INFLUENCING PHYSICAL MOTIONS

The next time you walk into your office and see eye rolls, crossed arms, and fidgeting, you are not just witnessing body language, you are experiencing the visual motions that foreshadow the upcoming actions of those people. Besides, you are not the only one seeing those nonverbal cues. The rest of the team encounters these dividing motions and will be impacted as well.

Like me, you would rather see people smiling, leaning in during a meeting, and nodding their heads in agreement as new goals and objectives are set. You would prefer to see people rubbing their hands together in anticipation of taking action. But you cannot bark orders or give ultimatums to make it happen. We cannot force people to make unifying physical motions but we can take two powerful steps to influence it.

Two Powerful Steps that Influence Action:

1. Train It
2. Model It

Train It:

We have already agreed that communication is the most critical element for successful businesses. Yet, we rarely see training sessions dedicated to speaking more effectively in the workplace environment. Hence, there is almost assuredly zero time dedicated to training people on the power of the physical motions they are making (and observing) in their environment. Body language is too important to merely hope people will learn how to use it properly.

Because our nonverbal cues may often communicate a more powerful message than our words and speeches, it makes sense to provide training sessions for our people. We need to teach the intentional and unintentional impact of their gestures. We can no longer afford to be ravaged by the storms of *dividing* body language. Foster an environment that protects your people and provides your entire team with *unifying* physical motions.

Training, on any subject, allows us to strengthen the skills of our people. Coaching our team members on the acceptable (firm handshakes) and unacceptable (crossed arms) body language in our businesses will reinforce their nonverbal skills. By prioritizing the team's understanding of physical motions, we not only increase their performance, but we eliminate any excuses for ignorance.

Sound Bite:
Consistent training is the key to teaching people how to utilize positive physical motions.

You cannot expect people to master something they are not taught. A lack of training sends the message that there is a lack of importance. As with all training sessions, the opportunity exists to make it as meaningful, relevant, and interactive as possible. When people role-play with body language, there can be a humorous component that occurs, especially when someone shares "dividing" body language, such as eye rolls, crossed arms, or negative posture. As you implement Body Language Training, follow the keys to effective training on nonverbal messages.

Keys to Training on Body Language:

1. Establish Purpose   – Improve communication
2. Identify Objectives   – Increase the unifying gestures
                           – Decrease the dividing gestures
3. Schedule Sessions   – Set regular dates and times
4. Encourage Participation – Create interactive involvement
5. Evaluate Performance   – Provide feedback to your people
6. Recognize Success   – Reward behaviors you want duplicated
                           (More on recognition in Chapter 12)

It is undeniable that well-trained people are critical to success. Properly arm your people with professional and consistent communication training so they understand that you are investing in them and their environment. Send the message that you understand the importance of the physical motions happening in your organization. Get your people speaking the same *body language.*

Model It:

Nothing speaks more loudly about the importance of a topic than the behavior of those encouraging it. If you say that attendance is important, don't be late. If you announce that attention to detail is critical, complete assignments properly. If you say that body language is important, model the behaviors you want to see. The physical motions exhibited by leaders influence team member behaviors far greater than any policy or procedure.

In addition to consistent training, *modeling* is a powerful way to teach and reinforce appropriate behaviors. Modeling occurs when someone witnesses behavior then imitates it. It is wise to regularly model *unifying* behavior because *dividing* behavior can also be modeled and imitated and take a stronghold in your workplace. Also referred to as observational learning or social learning, modeling does not require direct instruction or explanation – just the physical motions.

While the individual team member may be unaware that modeling is happening, influence is still occurring. You do not need a Ph.D. to teach body language – just *model* the right physical motions. Pick and choose your nonverbal gestures wisely because people are imitating you whether you are modeling it or not.

When we say that "people are our greatest asset," or that "teamwork is everything," we must reinforce our claims by showing the proper physical motions that align with those bold statements. Become keenly aware of exhibiting high levels of bearing – carry and conduct yourself with physical motions that encourage positive actions.

Human communication has made extensive use of body language since the beginning of time and it is happening in your business right now. It has been a critical element in building relationships but has long been overlooked and ignored in the workplace. Each person must identify the appropriate physical motions that are genuine and sincere ways of communicating for them.

I tend to give high-fives for the accomplishment of important tasks. I send a thumbs up to people who do their job with efficiency. A pat on the back allows me to show someone that I appreciate them. I nod, lean in, make eye contact, and purposefully set my phone down when people speak to me. I am aware of the message my posture sends. Even when I feel "down," my posture is "up."

Sound Bite:
Always be aware of the messages you are sending with your body language – someone is always interpreting them.

In the Marines, as the vice president of the media company, and as a business coach, I always have a "pep in my step" because even the way I walk sends a message to my team and my clients. When I say that we need a sense of urgency, I cannot afford to meander through the office. The gestures we make are paramount, not only to send messages but to be the example worth duplicating.

Our behaviors are always on display and we cannot avoid that, nor do we want to. Fortunately, to model body language effectively, we do not need to walk the runway at a fashion show. Instead, we need to focus on three elements to ensure that the physical motions we are exhibiting are understood and imitated properly.

The Three Elements of Modeling Body Language:

1. Understand MOTIVATION
2. Focus ATTENTION
3. Encourage DUPLICATION

Understand MOTIVATION: Each gesture sends a powerful message, so we need to identify the unifying body language we are going to model and define its meaning, leaving nothing to chance.

Focus ATTENTION: It is easy to get sidetracked and distracted at work, especially in an environment of *dividing* body language.

Be consistent with your nonverbal language and deliver unifying messages consistently.

Encourage DUPLICATION: Become natural in your physical motions so they do not seem awkward. Be the example worth duplicating. How you deliver your messages will entice people to start imitating your motions.

When it comes to communication, it is easy to say a few words with our voices but simultaneously send thousands of nonverbal messages with our bodies. People are already doing it in your organization. We can no longer witness the physical motions happening in our workplace and walk by. We must pay close attention to them, understanding the hidden meanings, and encourage more unifying gestures because every physical motion foreshadows *The Actions we Take.*

Communication Catalyst

Walking the Runway

Description: Select forms of body language to model, showing the impact of unifying and dividing nonverbal communication.

Time of Exercise: 60 minutes

Purpose: To identify the body language that should be used more in your organization and the body language that needs to be eliminated.

Resources: 3x5 cards, pens, white board, white board markers.

Presentation:

- Give a 3x5 card and a pen to each participant.
- Have each person list the body language, good and bad, that they have witnessed in the workplace.
- Go around and have each participant model body language, such as an eyeroll. Role play scenarios to show the impact of each instance of body language.
- Have an open discussion to describe the impact being made each time body language is used to communicate.
- Identify positive body language that needs to be incorporated into your workplace.

Debrief: This exercise is to be fun, while simultaneously showing the power of body language. Continue to discuss the impact of nonverbal communication. Teach the entire team the proper way to use body language and the types that need to be eliminated from the workplace.

Part IV

The ACTIONS We Take

You are what you do, not what you say you'll do.

~ Carl Jung

Part IV

The ACTIONS We Take

Each Action Reveals a Purpose.

How many times have you heard the old English adage, "A picture is worth a thousand words," meaning that a single still image may hold far more meaning than a verbal description? People tend to find the essence of the message in what they *see* rather than just what they *hear*. The saying has been modified to "An action is worth a thousand words," indicating that what we do may be significantly more important than what we say.

We've also likely heard an old proverb that has been translated from many different languages, "Actions speak louder than words." According to TheIdioms.com, "It was first recorded in English in this exact way. In 1736, in a piece of writing with the title, *Melancholy State of Province* the following is found: 'Actions speak louder than words and are more to be regarded.'"

The actions in your workplace are regarded as higher than the words spoken but is anyone paying attention? As the other old saying states, "It's not what you say, but what you do." So, all of these clichés are simply stating, at the end of the day, what you do is much more important than what you say. When our actions do not align with verbal and nonverbal communication, we not only live a lie but we divide people, instead of unifying them.

Sound Bite:
It takes very little time to say something but it requires effort to follow through and take action.

Why so much emphasis on *action*? While our words and speeches speak volumes, and we say so much with our body language, it is our actions that depict our true attitude and character, much more than our words, speeches, and gestures combined. Actions are more revealing of one's true intentions and set the stage for the level and quality of work in any organization.

Let's take a closer look at the definition of *action* so we can understand how to move our teams to take more of it and multiply their efforts.

ac · tion

noun

- a thing done; behaviors or conduct.
- the accomplishment of something usually over a period of time.
- the manner or method of performing.

Yes, our words, speeches, and gestures all significantly move our people but we deliver results based on the behaviors and performance of our team members, over a period of time. In the workplace, we must strive to accomplish more than everyone just doing their jobs. What if you could achieve teamwork, cohesion, and synergy? Would you rather achieve typical results using basic math (1 + 1 = 2) or mind-boggling results using "magnetic math" (1 + 1 = 4)?

INCREASING THE HORSEPOWER OF YOUR TEAM

When asked, most business leaders feel that their team members are capable of delivering more. Of course, that would be the logical response when so many people are *busy* and not *productive*. When I ask, "Can your people be more productive?" it is usually followed by a confident, "Absolutely!" Understand that the ability for higher levels of performance is not the issue – everyone knows it can be higher. The most common question I receive is, "How do we get them there?" I'm glad you asked.

According to the article, *How much weight can a horse pull? (You'll be surprised!)*, featured on HorseRookie.com, "pairing horses increases load capability, or how much weight they can pull together. If one horse can pull a cart weighing 6,000 lbs., two horses should be able to pull 12,000 lbs., right? If those horses are working together, they can actually pull 18,000 lbs. - three times the load one horse working alone can pull."

In other words, one plus one does not equal two, it equals three. This is precisely why we'll often see multiple horses pulling heavy loads. But it gets better when the horses have been trained together and perform with cohesion. When horses are unified the results are like *magnetic mathematics*.

A draft horse, also known as a workhorse, has been bred to plow fields, pull loads, and do other forms of labor. A single draft horse can pull up to 8,000 lbs. Based on the math above, two should pull three times as much – 24,000 pounds. But when they perform in tandem, working as a cohesive team, they have been able to pull up to 32,000 pounds – four times as much as the single horse.

Unfortunately, most business leaders fail to connect their people in a way that multiplies their efforts and are forced to hire more people to handle the workload. Imagine the possibilities of a magnetic team that is trained to speak the *Shared Language of Success* in your workplace. To do this, establish regular communication training sessions to harness the unlimited horsepower of your team, and allow them to display their true strength.

Sound Bite:
Increase the horsepower of your team by teaching them to work together as a cohesive unit.

OVERCOMING INERTIA

Plowing the fields is a critical *action* in farming. It digs deep into the soil, turning it over and improving the cultivation of the land. This provides the seeds with a higher chance of growing and germinating. Undoubtedly, the plow is a powerful and important tool but will merely remain motionless until it is hitched to a horse.

The law of inertia, also called Newton's first law, states that, if a body is at rest it will remain at rest unless it is acted upon by a force. The plow will be stuck in a state of dormancy until the farmer creates movement and attaches it to the horse. When status quo is allowed in the workplace, complacency sets in, and the unwillingness to "move" could take a stronghold in your environment.

in · er · tia

noun

- a tendency to do nothing or to remain unchanged.
- inactivity, sluggishness.
- resistance to motion, exertion.

When inertia exists in any part of a business, it is easy for people to feel stuck – motionless, stagnant, and status quo. Would you like to see your sales team be more productive? Does your operations team need to exhibit more initiative? Do the leaders need to do more proactive leading? If any parts of your business feel stuck, in the grasp of stagnation, then *actions* are the solutions to create intentional movement.

Because it is usually easier to stop something from happening than to exert the energy to make something happen, we must always be focused on *The Actions We Take* in the workplace and the actions our people take (and do not take). To overcome the devastating effects of inertia – complacency, laziness, procrastination – we must strive to achieve *synergy* with our actions.

According to the dictionary, *synergy* is combined action – the whole is greater than the sum of the parts. In other words, two synergistic team members will do the work of three, perhaps four. We know this happens when horses work together. It also occurs as sled dogs work together to pull their 300-400-pound sled during the 938-mile trek of the Iditarod Trail Sled Dog Race.

Geese, flying in a v-formation, experience reduced drag and can increase their range by 71% over a single goose. Dolphins, whales, lions, and wolves increase their results when hunting in packs. Bees work together for the common objectives within the hive and ants will even link their bodies together to form a bridge so the rest of the team can cross streams. The ants forming the bridge usually drown – that's commitment!

In each case, animals have learned that they can accomplish much more together than any single creature could alone – that is synergy! As a business coach, I have discovered that most organizations have barely scratched the surface of the synergy that is possible among their team members. If it works in the animal kingdom, imagine the possibilities in the business kingdom.

CONNECTING THE PIECES OF YOUR ACTION PUZZLE

When I began my career at the media company, in 2003, I watched people merely show up for work. While I did witness some hustle and initiative, it was sporadic, and not at the consistent levels we would need to accomplish the goal of "doubling sales." As if the goal of increasing sales was not enough, we also launched new post-production services, transitioned into the world of high-definition, and continued to operate through the Great Recession of 2007-2009.

It was not enough that people merely did their jobs or that departments operated at satisfactory levels within their silos. We needed to unify our entire team. We needed people working together, looking out for each other, and creating innovative ideas that would take us to new levels. We could not afford for each department to operate individually, with little regard for the other departments. We also needed each department to intentionally link together if we expected greater results.

Our goals were critically important to us and became an integral part of our vision. They were the puzzle pieces needed to complete our big picture. To allow those puzzle pieces to remain scattered on the floor would have been detrimental to our success. As a leader, I could not allow *inertia* to halt our movement. We needed action.

How important are your short-term and long-term business goals? How important are the objectives and enhancements you have envisioned for the future of your organization? If they are important, as I imagine they are, then you will need to focus on understanding the actions that are required to unify your team and create the geometric multiplication required for success.

Just as every word delivers *meaning*, each speech sends a *message*, and all gestures make an *impact*. Our actions reveal our *purpose*. If your purpose is to unify your people, then you will need to understand the four types of actions required to complete the *Action Puzzle* in the workplace.

The Four Pieces of the Action Puzzle:

1. Expected Actions
2. Planned Actions
3. Inspired Actions
4. Amplified Actions

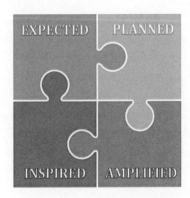

Expected Actions: The basic day-to-day expectations, like the duties and responsibilities listed in the job descriptions, that need to be completed.

Planned Actions: The tasks required to complete the goals detailed in the plan for the future growth of your organization.

Inspired Actions: The objectives that need to be attained from the innovative and creative ideas resulting from collaborative discussions.

Amplified Actions: The synergistic efforts occurring as a result of team cohesion, resulting in the magnification of performance (1 + 1 = 4).

The *Action Puzzle* allows us to identify the pieces currently being placed, and required to be placed, in our businesses to complete the unification of our people and magnify their results. The four actions happening in our business are vital, and we cannot complete the big picture by leaving one out.

There is also a piece of the *Action Puzzle* that does not belong. Although it is snugly fit into most workplace environments, *Divided Actions* do a significant amount of damage and alter the big picture of every organization. Keep this piece out of your puzzle.

Divided Actions: The minimal efforts, lack of attention to detail, subpar quality, and deficiency of enthusiasm while working (or not working).

To complete the Action Puzzle, it's time to recognize and enhance the actions in our workplace. To ensure that the actions of our people result in geometric multiplication, we are going to focus on the three outcomes of actions to further unify our people.

The Three Monumental Outcomes of our ACTIONS:

1. Synchronizing Performance
2. Harmonizing Efforts
3. Boosting Recognition

Communication Catalyst

Action Identifier

Description: List the actions you want to see happening more in the workplace.

Time of Exercise: 60 minutes

Purpose: To identify the actions that should be taken more, and the actions that need to go away in your organization.

Resources: 3x5 cards, pens, white board, white board markers.

Presentation:

- Give a 3x5 card and a pen to each participant.
- Ask participants to list as many actions as possible – actions to increase and actions to decrease.
- Go around and have each participant share their actions as someone lists each word on a white board. Using two columns, denote actions to increase and actions to decrease.
- Have an open discussion, identifying the impact of increasing the unifying actions and the impact of decreasing the dividing actions.
- Create a final list of all actions and the ways to increase unifying actions and eliminate dividing actions.

Debrief: Regularly reconnect with the team to assess the status of the actions being increased and those being decreased. Course-correct, as necessary.

Chapter 10

Synchronizing Performance

Systems Lead to High Levels of Teamwork.

For every action, there is a first step. "Forward march" was the initial command we heard in boot camp, signaling the recruits of Platoon 1095 to move ahead together. That was soon followed by "Left, right, left," which sounded simple enough. But performing each step to the expectations of our drill instructors was not as easy as one would think. Could we step down with our left foot, then our right, then our left? Of course, we could. But that was not the only objective.

There were forty-eight recruits in our platoon and our DI's expected us to step with flawless synchronization, each combat boot touching down as one. When we first learned to march, we sounded like a machine gun firing off dozens of rounds each time we took a step, rather than the single, explosive sound of a shotgun that they were looking for.

Was it possible to get all forty-eight recruits to sound like one; to move in unison? With much practice, and when I say much, I am talking about hours each day, we became a cohesive unit. We heard the commands "To the right, to the left, mark time, half step, and column of files" as we practiced throughout the day. The list goes on and on but we learned to execute each drill movement with precision and discipline.

Marching is an action that has a much deeper purpose than just troop movement. Although our drill instructors meticulously and repetitiously called *cadence*, the "call-and-response" marching commands that dictated our on-foot movements, walking was not the main point of military drill. Marching was necessary to create the cohesion required to achieve the highest levels of excellence – to unleash our maximum performance.

According to the Marine Corps Drill and Ceremonies Manual, which is over 550 pages, "The object of close-order drill is to teach Marines by exercise to obey orders and to do so immediately in the correct way. Close order drill is one foundation of discipline and esprit de corps. Additionally, it is still one of the finest methods for developing confidence and troop leading abilities in our subordinate leaders."

In ancient times, troop movement was essential for winning battles. Powerful empires developed their own unique ways of moving their soldiers from one strategic location to the next without confusing the commanders or mixing up their troops. It was paramount that the soldiers did not get lost on the way to the battle and end up fighting alongside random units. Victory had a greater chance when they could fight with those they trained with and achieve *synergy* (1 + 1 = 4).

Today's military units have access to many forms of troop transportation, everything from helicopters and airplanes, to trucks and Humvees. Yet, every man and woman currently serving are taught to march as soon as they start basic training. So, why is there still such a keen focus on drill in each branch of the armed services? Marching is one of the fundamental team-building skills in the military. This is the first step to unification.

Sound Bite:
Marching is not about walking better; it is about performing better.

While drill is still performed at military ceremonies and parades, the purpose is much greater than looking sharp in front of a crowd. At the end of the day, each branch of service prepares for war. Discipline in battle is crucial for both survival and victory. Marching is an *Expected Action* for *synchronizing performance* and provides service members with specific benefits on the drill field and in every facet of their day-to-day work.

The Benefits of Actions that Synchronize Performance:

- Demonstrates the need to act as part of a team.
- Allows team movements to be effective and efficient.
- Encourages actions to be repeated until they are second nature.
- Instills discipline in following commands quickly.
- Makes a unit look formidable.
- Allows the team to perform under challenging circumstances.

We were not taught to walk, but rather to march together as a team – a cohesive unit. While marching is not mastered quickly, it is an action that clearly builds unit discipline and confidence, translating into the rest of our daily actions. In your business, you deserve to have this level of teamwork, too, and it is absolutely possible to achieve this in the workplace with civilians.

SYNCHRONIZING YOUR TEAM

You run a business, not a military command, so, you cannot implement marching in your organization. Asking your people to "fall in" while you shout drill commands at them probably will not go over well. Like most business professionals, you see the need for greater levels of cohesion, discipline, attention to detail, effectiveness, efficiency, and pride with your people. Now, it's time to take the *actions* required to achieve them.

While I believe that team cohesion is one-hundred percent attainable in the business sector, I am often asked, "Where do I start?" We achieved synergy at the media company without ever calling cadence. I now help my clients to do it without ever once stepping onto the drill field. And you can do it, too, as long you take the *actions* required to synchronize team performance.

Leading my media team, I could feel it when we were operating "in sync" and I could feel it when we were not. I'm confident that the rest of our team could feel it, too, and I'm certain that our clients also felt it. The importance of increasing our cohesion was necessary if we expected to accomplish our short-term and long-term goals.

Since marching was not an option for synchronizing our efforts, I began to look for ways to unify us. I searched for something that would have a similar effect to marching; something that would unify each department; something that would synchronize every person in our company. I quickly discovered that our systems had the power to create increased discipline and confidence while allowing us to simultaneously provide the greatest results.

One of the biggest complaints among people in the business sector is the lack of attention to detail from their co-workers – those who do "most" of the work but not "all" of it. Frustrations occur when time frames are not met, steps are ignored, signatures are missing, and supporting documents are absent. I replaced drill movements with system actions to synchronize our performance.

When we processed orders at the media company, each project passed through multiple departments and was touched by at least a dozen team members. The possibilities for errors were high, especially when each videotape we duplicated had thousands of frames and multiple audio channels, not including any additional technical specifications and labeling instructions that came with each unique order.

The individual steps taken by each team member were critical but their ability to successfully transition each order to the next department was paramount. We could not afford to hear our people say, "It's not my job," or "This is just the way I do it," if we expected success. Our efforts needed to be synchronized from one person to the next. We could not perform as five separate departments; we needed to perform as one, with each person taking steps with flawless synchronization.

When I started at the media company, we processed about 500 orders per month with 15% of our orders having internal mistakes, caused by our team members, which resulted in a "re-do." An error was not just bad for completing the order correctly and delivering it on time, but it also negatively impacted our reputation. Although we had some standard operating procedures and guidelines for completing orders, I soon realized that everyone was doing things differently, albeit slightly.

By creating our systems, we synchronized team performance, allowing us to increase the number of orders we processed to over 1,200 per month and also raised the volume of each order. As our annual sales revenue grew to over 300%, we also launched a second facility in Burbank and began taking orders from New York and Europe. We were also transitioning our entire operation from standard definition to high definition, building out cutting-edge editorial bays, and adding new services like closed-captioning and digital restoration.

We also expanded our hours of operation. Originally open from 9:00 am to 7:00 pm, we eventually operated with three shifts, around the clock. Any one of these variables could increase the likelihood of additional mistakes. But our internal errors went down, and not by a little. We watched our "re-do" ratio plummet significantly, from 15% to .35%. Yes, there is a point in front of the "35." We not only increased our sales results, but we nearly eliminated every mistake caused by our people. We synchronized performance by focusing our actions on our systems.

Sound Bite:
Systems provide businesses with the steps to synchronize the performance of their people.

You will not have the luxury of marching to build high levels of teamwork but you do have a viable solution to strengthen the cohesion of your people – your systems. If your goals are important to you, then synchronizing the performance of your team will be the optimal pathway for success. To do that, you need to align their actions with the steps in your systems.

YOUR TEAM RUNS YOUR SYSTEMS

While each branch of service has its own color guard, the Joint-Service Color Guard is made up of service members from the Army, Navy, Air Force, Coast Guard, and Marine Corps. They synchronize their performance to represent our nation, show unity, and honor our flag. While they are all from different branches, they understand drill movements and *speak* the shared language fluently.

In business, this would be the same as having a person from each of your departments work together in unison with every step they take to operate your systems. Imagine having systems that connect each department while your team members execute each movement in seamless unison. That is the level of teamwork we reached at the media company. It was not always easy to get our actions to be synchronized but it was always worth it.

Because communication transmits a message between the sender and the receiver, we cannot afford to overlook the actions that deliver powerful messages to our people. In the workplace, our actions reveal our true intentions and significantly impact our ability to move our people – to synchronize performance. Systems do more than just enhance the skills of your people and reduce mistakes, they bridge the gap between departments, allowing everyone to perform in sync.

McDonald's may not be known for having one of the best burgers in town, but they are known for having one of the best systems in business. The Speedee Service System, launched in 1948, by brothers Richard and Maurice McDonald, lead to their "drive-in" concept, franchising opportunities, and eventually caught the eye of Ray Kroc, who became their first franchise agent in 1954. Ray Kroc bought out the McDonald brothers, in 1961, for $2.7 million, and turned their system into a worldwide corporation now valued at over $150 billion.

How important is running a system to McDonald's? Their current systems are now taught at Hamburger University, their training facility located in Chicago, Illinois. Their motto is *Learning Today, Leading Tomorrow* and their corporate university has trained and graduated more than 80,000 managers, mid-managers, and owner-operators to run their systems and understand all aspects of restaurant management.

UNDERSTANDING THE DEEPER PURPOSE OF SYSTEMS

A system is a series of interconnected processes that dictate how people complete the "steps" of a project, order, or task. These steps are already being taken every day in our businesses, but when they are left to chance, we miss out on the power of creating synergy. Unfortunately, many people accomplish things based on the information in their heads or they have modified the existing system slightly because "This is how I've always done it." Without a unified system, our people will continue to "march" out of sync.

The use, or misuse, of our systems is an integral part of our daily communication with our people. Each action, or the lack of action, sends a powerful message about our commitment to excellence, quality, and teamwork. When it comes to systems there are many types, including the ones listed below.

Types of Business Systems:

- Sales System
- Accounting System
- Marketing System
- On-Boarding System
- Payroll System
- Operations System
- HR System
- Strategic Planning System
- Training System
- Customer Service System

Each system is the collection of the "steps" required to complete the assignment successfully. My Sales Impact System (SIS) combines the following steps: prospecting, contacting, presenting, set-up, and follow-up. The system identifies the best practices for each step then seamlessly connects them so the whole is greater than the sum of the parts – synergy!

Systems allow us to work smarter, not harder. They are the building blocks of predictable efficiency and play a significant role in the success of any business. Because our systems are run by our people, every action is important, and we need them to be synchronized. When they are off the mark, it can have a devastating impact on the team and the customers.

Sound Bite:
Your systems increase efficiencies by allowing your people to march to the beat of the same drum.

In boot camp, we were all taught to step off with our left foot after the command, "Forward, march." Every service member in every branch of service understands that basic first step. Imagine what would happen if some failed to step off and some opted to step off with their right foot, while the rest stepped off with their left foot. Chaos! Yes, movement would happen but it would not be as effective as *synchronized performance*.

Systems are completely worthless without the actions of our team members. Creating and implementing systems increase our ability for success but success is based on how our people take action. When it comes to the actions associated with running systems, there are three that impact the success we achieve.

Three System Actions that Impact Success:

1. No Action   - Steps are left to chance
2. Optional Action   - Steps are only suggestions
3. Synchronized Action - Steps are executed flawlessly

No Action:

When the steps in our systems are not enforced, or perhaps not even clearly identified, we leave our results to chance. Hoping that people take the right action is not a viable strategy. When no system is in place, it sends the message that attention to detail is not valued and failures are tolerated.

Optional Action:

When steps are merely suggestions, we create unnecessary conflict within our team. Having a system only as a guideline allows for too many variations of your "best practices." It also sends the message that people can choose what *feels* right for them over what *is* right for the team.

Synchronized Action:

When steps are executed flawlessly, we not only increase our chances for success but we significantly reduce errors and frustrations. Enforcing our systems improves team performance while sending the message of unification, cohesion, synchronization.

Without a doubt, it is less expensive to create and run a workflow than it is to fix mistakes. How we run our systems communicates volumes to our people. When I explain the benefits of incorporating or enhancing processes into the workplace, I like to draw a parallel to the medical industry. My wife has battled four different types of cancers and she suffered cardiac arrest, died for fifteen minutes, and was brought back to life after a week in the ICU.

I prefer to take her to hospitals that have *synchronized performance* among their team members. I like to know that the actions they take are not merely options but are proven to work. It reassures me to know that she will not be randomly moved from room to room, and I feel better knowing that everyone is part of the team and they are committed to taking the steps in their system flawlessly.

Would you go to a hospital with optional steps or no steps at all? When lives are at stake, systems make perfect sense. In business, livelihoods are at stake and our actions should be focused on running our systems. Not only will it unify our people but the effect will be felt by our customers. The benefits of creating, implementing, and running systems are too great to ignore.

The Benefits of Synchronized Systems:

- Eliminate Redundancies
- Streamline Communication
- Increase Accountability
- Enhance Satisfaction
- Deliver Results
- Magnify Performance
- Elevate Morale

LET YOUR TEAM IN ON THE ACTION!

By now, you are hopefully "all-in" on running systems at the highest levels of excellence. At the media company, we did not have formal systems in place when I started there. This became our opportunity to create them together as a team. The action of building our systems was unifying. If you have systems in place, there is no time like now to enhance them – with your people. If you do not have systems in place, there is no time like now to design them – with your people.

When I ask leaders if they have systems, most quickly respond with "Yes," but then struggle to show me the detailed steps they "hope" their people use to maximize results. In some cases, businesses have outgrown their current workflows – their company grew but their systems did not. At the media company, our systems needed to be refined as our sales, services, and the team continued to expand.

Including your team in the creation or enhancement of your systems increases their buy-in and communicates to them how much you value their insights. After all, they already know the gaps that cause high levels of unnecessary mistakes that lead to unwanted stress and frustration. So, you can enlist their help to identify the steps for success – the actions to synchronize performance.

Allowing my entire team at the media company to participate in the creation, implementation, and enhancement of our systems, had a significant impact on everyone. Systems do more than show how things should be done. They bring people together to perform as a team. Our actions affect our people by unifying or dividing them.

- Unifying Actions: Creating a system and running it
- Dividing Actions: Guessing at the steps and winging it

Designing a deliberate system with your people gives them a distinct advantage in the workplace. Efficient processes keep everyone on the same page (of the workflow) and speaking the same language (steps in each system). Systems reduce confusion, stress, redundancies, and miscommunication.

Sound Bite:
Streamlining the way things are done is beneficial to everyone.

KEEPING IT SIMPLE

When leaders think about designing a new system or enhancing an existing one, some quickly become overwhelmed. I always ask the same question, "What takes more time, running a system or fixing a mistake?" A mistake can occur in a second but repairing it may take hours, days, or even weeks. Besides, the cost of making one mistake may far outweigh the cost of creating a predictable system.

Although we initially lacked a well-defined system for processing our orders at the media company, we did have many "System Successes" – examples of work being completed, from start to finish without any mistakes. Because every success leaves clues that can be repeated, we built our systems around the connection of the successful steps happening inside each department and in between each department.

As we formulated our system for work orders, our leaders meticulously followed numerous orders through the "System" and made the necessary enhancements. Our team not only contributed to the fine-tuning of our procedures but they witnessed the leaders taking action to create a system that synchronized our performance. That action communicated a powerful message to the team as we began "marching" together to successfully complete each step in our system.

To further multiply the understanding and power of the system, we made everything visual. This reinforced the importance of the system and increased the retention of each step. We added further clarification by featuring one-page "Checkpoints" in each department, clearly listing all of the steps to "march" the order forward. We also provided a color-coded workflow of how each step in our systems, for services ranging from video duplication and DVD replication to editorial and restoration, should be completed. These became our steps for success.

The checkpoints and the thirty-two color-coded workflow charts were added to our training schedules and we "drilled for skill" on how to synchronize our team performance. Our system connected all of the steps from one department to the next. The transition steps, between each department, became a huge focal point for us. This is where we needed flawless communication and unparalleled cohesion. We needed teamwork.

Each system (sales, operations, HR, etc.) allows your team to do what they are already doing, but more effectively and efficiently. Most importantly, every step in your system is an action that communicates unification throughout your organization. When the performance of your people is synchronized, their movements lead to synergistic results.

It's a great feeling when work is completed without mistakes. But it is an even greater feeling when our people act as a cohesive unit, working together to overcome challenges, empower each other, and deliver excellence. Systems provide us with the opportunity to consistently take steps toward greatness – to march in unison.

BUSINESS IS LIKE A GAME OF CHESS

My dad taught me how to play chess as a child, and while I am no Grandmaster, I enjoy the strategy involved in playing and winning. It did not take me long to realize that every move had significant implications on the outcome of the game! In business, like in chess, every action has significant implications on the outcome of your success.

Tactics are integral to the game of chess and it comes as no surprise that volumes of books have been written about them and YouTube has thousands of instructional videos uploaded about how to play the game. Unfortunately, there are far fewer resources available to business leaders to understand how to tactically "move" and win at business.

Make no mistake that every move, every action taken, not only communicates a message to our people, but they also position our team to succeed! We need to treat every action as a tactical chess move, one that has the potential to either cost us the game or to allow us to victoriously communicate "Checkmate."

The challenge of playing chess is learning how to think strategically (long-term) while making tactical moves (short-term). But this is the same challenge we face in business. Every tactical action taken now can have severe implications on our strategic objectives later. Like chess, we must concentrate on our moves to fully initiate *The COMMUNICATION Movement*.

In business, as in chess, we take proactive and reactive actions. Every action impacts the game and can open or close the next opportunity for our people. Actions can lead to gaining or losing business, retaining or replacing leaders, hiring or firing team members, increasing or decreasing margins, earning a new contract, or watching it go to your competitor. Every action should increase our chances of winning.

Just like in chess, keep a watchful eye on every move being made, understanding the meaning and implications. Determine your actions carefully – there is a lot at stake.

Communication Catalyst

System Support

Description: Identify ways to enhance and support your business systems.

Time of Exercise: 60 minutes

Purpose: Recognize the systems in place and how to improve them. List the systems still needed.

Resources: 3x5 cards, pens, white board, white board markers.

Presentation:

- Give a 3x5 card and a pen to each participant.
- Ask participants to list the current systems used in your work environment – all departments.
- Go around and have each participant share their ideas on how to improve the current systems in place, such as refining specific steps, removing redundancies, and/or enhancing communication.
- Next, ask participants to list the systems still needed to be implemented for increased efficiencies and teamwork.
- Create a list of actions to enhance or create your systems.

Debrief: Regularly meet with your team to discuss system enhancements, reevaluating periodically to ensure high levels of efficiency. Provide consistent training and cross-training on your systems to ensure that your people are completing each step in your systems.

Chapter 11

Harmonizing Efforts

Getting Your Team to Play in Tune!

"Lights, camera, action!" Even though this phrase is never used on a movie set, we all know that the director sets the tone for everyone working on the film and ultimately announces when the action begins. Typically, you will hear commands like "Quiet on the set, roll sound, roll camera...." But another command is also used before "Action."

When "Slate" is said, the clapboard is placed in front of the camera and struck together. The "clap" is identified visually on the film and the sound is heard distinctly on the audio recording. This allows for the much-needed synchronization of the picture and the sound. When they fail to align, even slightly, it can be highly noticeable. An actor's lips that do not match the words are distracting, hindering the audience's experience and pulling them out of the moment.

In filmmaking, synchronizing the visuals and the sounds is critical but there is another form of unification that is necessary to complete the final product – achieving harmony among the cast and crew throughout each creative step. Filmmaking is a collaborative process, that continues through all three phases. The **pre-production** phase is all about planning and preparing. The script is broken down into individual scenes, locations are locked in, props are identified, and costumes are designed.

The **production** phase is where principal photography takes place. The lighting of the set occurs, and the scenes are rehearsed so everyone is ready for "Action." As the shooting is completed, the film enters the **post-production** phase, which includes editing, sound mixing, and special effects. Whew! That's a lot of moving parts and a lot of people are required to move them.

To say that teamwork is essential in filmmaking is a huge understatement. Just take a look at the credits of a feature film to see how many people are involved, sometimes from around the world. The end credits of *Avengers Endgame* lasted twelve minutes. There were thousands of people involved in the creation of one project. Numerous individuals, all harmonizing their efforts to complete one movie. *Avengers Endgame* went on to earn $2,797,800,564 at the worldwide box office.

WORKPLACE HARMONY

How many people are needed to complete projects in your business? While you will likely not need as many as it takes to make a major motion picture, you will still benefit from a team that operates well together. I have discovered that it always takes a team to succeed, and that team needs to have its efforts operating in harmony.

Sound Bite:
Teamwork does not happen by putting people together, it happens when they create harmony together.

When we think of harmony, we naturally think about music. Defining it, an orchestra comes to mind, especially as we logically connect these two definitions from the dictionary:

- The combination of simultaneous musical notes in a chord.
- The structure of music with respect to the composition.

Both descriptions make sense when you consider tuning your musical instruments. Vocal harmony can also be achieved as two or more singers layer their voices with each other. According to HarmonyHelper.com, "Many of the singers we've interviewed describe the experience of singing harmonies as causing a physical sensation almost like a buzzing when they're getting it right."

Like most business professionals, you want your people to "get it right" and feel the "buzz" at work, perhaps more than they are currently doing. Do some fall flat when they could be hitting the sweet sound of success? You and your people deserve to experience harmony through your efforts. But is it possible to achieve harmony in the workplace? Well, when you look up *Workplace Harmony* on Google there are 24.8 million results that come back.

While that is a lot of information to sift through, it is one-hundred percent achievable. At the media company, we were involved in the post-production phase of the entertainment industry – movies, TV shows, and commercials. When we harmonized our efforts, and our actions were in-tune, we produced greater results. To achieve *harmony*, in the layered activities of our people, let's look deeper into the other definitions of this "moving" word.

har · mo · ny

noun

- the combination of simultaneous notes to produce a pleasing effect.
- a pleasing arrangement of parts.
- an interweaving of different accounts into a single narrative.

Ok, now we're talking! To experience *Business Harmony*, we need to constantly strive for the *pleasing effect of simultaneous notes (actions) as we arrange our people to form a single narrative*. It's all about harmonizing the efforts of our people. Imagine the possibilities when your team harmonizes their efforts on every goal, objective, task, and project.

While everyone in the military is taught to synchronize their performance when they march, there is an elite team that marches in the Marine Corps without any verbal commands. Without cadence, The Marnie Corps Silent Drill Platoon executes a series of calculated drill movements, far beyond the basic marching techniques we learned in boot camp.

Since they first performed in 1948, this highly disciplined 24-man platoon tours the world and exemplifies the professionalism associated with the Corps. While there are no verbal commands, the sounds created by their feet stepping down and their hands moving their rifles, create a powerful and pleasing sound – they achieve harmony through their actions.

Being part of a great team is a phenomenal experience. When people operate in harmony, they are "in the zone," accomplishing more, and feeling energized, even when faced with challenges. The actions happening in your environment will determine if your business is a box office blockbuster or a box office bomb.

CAUTION: CONFLICT AHEAD

Music is comprised of three main elements—melody, rhythm, and *harmony*. While the first two help to make the music memorable, it is the third element, harmony, that can transform it from average to great. Remember, harmony is the combined effect when all of the individual notes and voices form a cohesive whole.

In the workplace. we achieve business harmony as the combined performance of our people form a whole that is better than the individual efforts of a single person. In an orchestra, a flutist plays one note, a trumpeter hits another note, while the violinist plays the third note. As each of their musical notes are heard at the same time, it creates harmony. When music is pleasing to the ear it is known as *consonance* – sounds, that when played together complement each other.

When music is unpleasing, it is often caused by a clashing of two or more notes that do not fit well together. This is known as *dissonance* and creates feelings of discomfort and annoyance. In the workplace, the actions our people take together need to cause *consonance* (be pleasing). If we fail to harmonize the actions of our people, this can result in dissonance (be unpleasing).

Workplace harmony is *the combined effort of our people, resulting in a pleasing outcome.* Given the option of a pleasing outcome or an unpleasing outcome, I am certain that everyone in the workplace would choose pleasing. So, why does it not exist in most businesses? It's difficult to reach harmony when 68% of our people are not engaged (per the statistics from Gallup) but not impossible.

Conflict is one major challenge that hinders our efforts to achieve harmony. Does conflict exist in your business? It probably does when 14% of the workforce is actively disengaged. As you and I both know, it may only take one person to disrupt the applecart and create dissonance in our organizations. Harmony is difficult to maintain in conflicting environments. So, let's take a closer look at the biggest roadblock for harmonizing efforts – conflict.

con · flict

noun/verb

- to come into collision or disagreement.
- to be contradictory.
- a fight, battle, or struggle.
- a discord of action.

Are you seeing everything come together in *The COMMUNICATION Movement*? Take another look at the fourth definition of conflict – a *discord of action.* Taking a closer look at the definition of *discord,* we find that it is: *a lack of **harmony** between persons.* Conflict can occur between two people, two departments, two leaders, and even two owners. No matter who it occurs between the conflict impacts the efforts of everyone who encounters it.

Sound Bite:
Conflict in the workplace is like an iceberg to the Titanic – best not to ignore it.

While *Workplace Harmony* had 24.8 million results, I also searched *Workplace Conflicts* on Google and found over 100 million more results – 129,000,000, to be exact. Based on these numbers, I am guessing that there is much more conflict in the workplace than harmony. That was the exact scenario when I started at the media company – more conflicting efforts than harmonizing efforts with our people.

THE IMPACT OF CONFLICTING ACTIONS

As a business coach, I can wholeheartedly confirm that there is way too much unnecessary conflict in the workplace. Sometimes, tensions are so high, I can quickly detect it when I step into the environments of my clients for the first time. They become undeniable when I conduct assessments of their leaders and team members. I have yet to meet anyone who admitted to wanting conflict at work, so who's authorizing it in so many businesses?

I have never seen "Bring the highest levels of conflict and negatively impact the efforts of your co-workers" in anyone's job descriptions. I do not recall attending training sessions on "Achieving More Conflict," nor have I studied workflow charts detailing the steps necessary for "Conflict Creation." No one has ever been hired to cause conflict but it certainly permeates the fibers of most organizations.

In addition to sucking up a significant amount of time, negatively impacting team morale, reducing the effectiveness of performance, and hurting the bottom-line, conflicting actions divide our people. They push them away and make harmony nearly impossible to achieve. Below are some of the factors that lead to conflict in the workplace.

Factors That Cause Workplace Conflict:

- Egos
- Pride
- Jealousy
- Negativity
- Lack of Teamwork
- Subpar Communication
- Department Silos

- Opposing Positions
- Favoritism
- Power Struggles
- Drama
- Low Expectations
- Lack of Performance
- Poor Leadership

The list can go on and on but to navigate the stormy seas of conflict, we cannot ignore them. We need to be aware of any factor that can impact the cohesion of our people. Conflict, however, is not isolated only to the business sector. Did you know that it exists in the military, too? Because our troops are also in the "people" business, conflict can arise among their fellow service members, not just from the enemy. In both cases, as a Marine, I learned that it should be addressed promptly and professionally.

Unresolved conflict can lead to feelings of stress, frustration, unhappiness, and dissatisfaction. Because we are all in the "people" business, some levels of conflict are a natural part of every workplace environment. But we need to get it in check. While the idea of creating a perfect utopia sounds nice, it is not realistic. For harmony to thrive, we must manage our current conflicts, while eliminating future incidents.

Sound Bite:
For workplace harmony to thrive, manage current conflicts, and eliminate future ones.

RESOLVING CONFLICT

When conflict occurs, it's not uncommon to hear leaders say, "I have better things to do than babysit a bunch of adults <u>acting</u> like children."

Conflict does not typically spring up overnight. It evolves, usually, as conflict-causing factors are overlooked or ignored. While it will not go away overnight, you will make progress by consistently taking the right actions.

In business, too many people fear conflict and tend to use avoidance as their solution, hoping it will go away. When conflict arises, it impacts the actions of our team members, and instead of harmony, we experience a *collision* with our people, just as the first definition of conflict pointed out.

No matter what resource you use to battle conflict, it is not uncommon for leaders to be advised to act fairly and swiftly. There are numerous ways to handle it, with thousands of techniques listed on the internet alone. Sometimes referred to as *dispute resolution*, you can be trained to handle conflict or even hire a consultant to come in and address it. Unfortunately, most "solutions" are typically temporary fixes. To unify our people, we need a permanent solution.

At the media company, I was involved in every type of conflict that arose between our team members, our leaders, and our clients. My objective was to avoid a repeat of the same situation in the future. There were ten essential keys I used to not only resolve an existing conflict but to steer it toward harmony.

10 Essential Keys to Conflict Resolution:

1. **Hit it Head-On:** When we wait and hope it goes away, we send the message of tolerating conflict. Address it quickly for the good of the entire team.
2. **Open Communication:** Initiating honest dialogue allows people to share more than just their feelings. Encourage people to express the truth about the conflicting incident.
3. **Listen like a Champ:** Ask questions but listen more to discover the root of the conflict. Building trust will empower people to share more about the real issues at hand.

4. **Put Yourself in Their Shoes:** There are always two sides to every story. Seek out the factual story and exhibit empathy when trying to understand what is causing the conflict.

5. **Exhibit Justice:** Stick to the facts. Be fair and consistent in determining your resolution. Never allow favoritism to sway your judgment.

6. **Find the Lesson**: While every conflict is challenging, they all provide an opportunity to avoid future incidents. Find the small agreements that can be made between both parties to unify the people experiencing (or causing) a conflict.

7. **Implement Training:** Every form of conflict provides a training opportunity dedicated to educating people and teaching them how to avoid falling into (or causing) future conflicts.

8. **Emotional Check:** It's easy for emotions to run high during conflicts, so you are best off to stay calm, cool, and collective to achieve the greatest results for resolution.

9. **Define Non-Negotiables:** Identify the acceptable behaviors and actions expected in your organization and establish a zero-tolerance policy for anything that conflicts with them.

10. **Lead by Example:** Everyone is watching what you do and what you neglect to do. The actions you take will be duplicated, so make sure yours are harmonious.

In any conflict scenario, like me, you will likely use many of the ten essential keys. While I completely agree with acting fairly and swiftly when conflict occurs, I'd like to suggest another approach. At the media company, I developed a proactive technique to avoid fostering an environment of conflict in the first place.

PREVENTING CONFLICT

Everyone deserves workplace harmony and you would probably agree that it is better to prevent conflict, rather than trying to resolve it. That is why I feel strongly about guiding our actions toward one powerful step that proactively positions you and your team to minimize potential conflict from rising at all. It's time to fully unify your team while also guarding against the hazards of unwanted conflict.

The 1 Unifying Step to Prevent Conflict:

1. **Implement Harmonizing Actions:** That's it, just one step? I know, it's so simple, right? The actions required to harmonize the efforts of your people will simultaneously squash conflict while bringing them together as a cohesive unit.

Dynamic and harmonious teamwork is commonplace in the military, sports, and the movie industry. But it is not limited to these three professions. It can flow in your environment too, as you implement the proper actions. If it makes sense that we need team-building actions to reap the benefits of teamwork, then it is also fair to say that we will need harmonizing actions to enjoy the pleasing results of consistent workplace harmony.

At the media company, I needed to reinvent myself if I expected to blaze a trail to greatness, especially as we were occasionally being detoured by conflict. As I rose from entry-level scheduler to vice president, I harmonized the efforts of our entire team. Together, we achieved over 300% sales growth and nearly eliminated all of our internal errors. The more we removed the distractions of conflict, the more we experienced the power of harmony.

Sound Bite:
Conflict must be eliminated if we expect to enjoy the benefits of harmony.

To ensure that workplace harmony was consistently flowing with our team, I combined my experiences as an air traffic controller in the Marine Corps, my sales skills from the financial services arena, and my knowledge of the movie industry.

Like the three phases of filmmaking, harmony also has three distinct components to ensure that it does not happen randomly by chance, but intentionally by choice. I developed, implemented, and maintained these phases to foster an environment where harmony was commonplace and conflict was foreign.

The Three Phases of Workplace Harmony:

1. Pre-Harmony
2. Harmony
3. Post-Harmony

Phase 1 – Pre-Harmony:

How we "set the stage" will have a significant impact on what we achieve. Pre-harmony allows us to establish high expectations and create an atmosphere where people can work together and achieve excellence, from the beginning of their journey with our businesses. Here are the actions necessary during the pre-harmony phase:

1. **First Contact:** The interviewing and hiring phase allows us to convey the "feel" of our environment. We need to hire people to our culture, rather than basing our decisions on the need for a "warm body" or solely on their well-written resumé.
2. **On-Boarding:** Often overlooked in most companies, this is a critical step in how we introduce people to their fellow team members, our systems, and how our team operates together. We cannot afford to have a "sink or swim" program to bring new people in and get them up to speed.
3. **Everyone is in Sales:** From the beginning, everyone needs to know that they are there to "share" or to support sales. At the media company, we began every job description with, "To support the sales goals by..." (and then the uniqueness of their

actual job was added). This unified our people with a common understanding of their core purpose.

Phase 2 – Harmony:

We have set the stage to create harmony and now it's time to experience it consistently. While everyone needs to understand that they are a very important cog, we are still just one cog. All the cogs are required to move our business machine. Harmonizing efforts allow us to act as a cohesive unit, relying on each other to support and strengthen teamwork. Here are the actions necessary during the harmony phase:

1. **Team Activities:** Our team is at its strongest when everyone is gathered. Off-site activities such as family picnics, book clubs, playing games/sports, and team meetings to share success stories, help to foster an environment of teamwork. Like we did at the media company, you may want to order lunches as achievements are made. Allow time for people to sit with each other. Slow down and get to know fellow team members.
2. **Team Cultivation:** Training – Cross-Training – Development! The full gambit of growing our team includes regular and relevant job training, cross-training sessions, and leadership development. If silos exist, cross-training between departments allows team members to "walk a mile in each other's shoes," breaking down the imaginary walls that do not actually exist but have the potential to deliver a significant amount of damage.
3. **Team Focus:** Working on common goals is essential for every successful team. Rallying people around shared goals allows them to channel their energies toward building deeper levels of trust, instead of getting caught up in the whirlwind of conflict. Teams with high levels of trust have higher levels of cohesion.

Sound Bite:
Teamwork is never high when trust is low.

Phase 3 – Post-Harmony:

Congratulations on achieving harmony. Now, we need to maintain it. Once harmony is flowing, the door is opened to actions that will sky-rocket the performance and results of your team. Post-harmony allows us to move our "harmonized" people into a position to achieve greater results. Here are the actions necessary during the post-harmony phase:

1. **Collaborating:** The act of creating innovative and creative solutions is nearly impossible to accomplish during a conflict. When our team performs in harmony, they can set aside egos and focus on the extraordinary ideas that will take our businesses to new levels.
2. **Strategic Planning:** Every business needs a plan to place and sort all the collaborative ideas generated from the team. The action of creating and implementing a plan sends a powerful message of forward movement, allowing the team to stay focused today as they work together for a better tomorrow. Remember to acknowledge WIIFM – What's In It For Me?
3. **Sharing Vision:** A lack of vision leads to aimlessness and wasted time in the workplace – leaving room for conflict to arise. Sharing the future vision for your organization provides a much-needed look ahead. Vision provides direction and purpose to a team operating in harmony, creating a rallying point for the entire team to say, "Let's go!"

Each of the *Three Phases of Workplace Harmony* is designed to run congruently – one is no more critical than the next. Your vision, for example, will be embraced deeper by a team operating with harmony, but sharing it during the interview and onboarding steps will bring everything full circle. We need to focus our actions on *harmonizing efforts* because a gap in these actions will cause the notes of harmony to fade away.

We now understand the unifying possibilities of *Synchronizing Performance* and *Harmonizing Efforts* in our teams. Is there something we can do to enhance *The COMMUNICATION Movement* even more? I'm glad you asked. It's time to focus on another action that will boost the unification of our people and allow them to fluently speak the *Shared Language of Success.*

Communication Catalyst

Conflict Crushers

Description: Identify and eliminate the unnecessary conflicts in your business.

Time of Exercise: 60 minutes

Purpose: To empower people to proactively resolve and eliminate situations that increase conflict among team members.

Resources: 3x5 cards, pens, white board, white board markers.

Presentation:

- Give a 3x5 card and a pen to each participant.
- Ask participants to list any conflicts they have seen arise in the workplace.
- Go around and have each participant share their experience with the conflicts they listed and what the impact has been on the team.
- Have an open discussion, identifying ways to resolve conflicts that currently exist.
- Identify the *Harmonizing Actions* that will prevent future conflicts.

Debrief: Regularly communicate *Harmonizing Actions* to ensure an environment with minimal conflicts. When conflict arises, face it immediately and with a plan to resolve it. Promptly discuss any new conflicts that arise to set the precedent of resolving conflict promptly.

Chapter 12

Boosting Recognition

Paying Attention Pays Off.

"Daddy, daddy, daddy, daddy, daddy." I heard the first "Daddy" from both of my sons and my daughter when they were young, but they always felt compelled to repeat my name until they had my full attention. My grandson, Mason, has his own special name for me. He loves to say "Pop-Pop, watch me" or "Pop-Pop, look at me" every time he jumps, runs, throws a ball, or pretty much does anything. He's not interested in just some of Pop-Pop's attention, he wants it all.

There is no denying that children need attention from adults. The right amount helps them to grow, develop self-esteem, form a positive self-image, accomplish tasks, and eventually succeed in life. Children crave attention, and while their repetitive dialogue may sometimes grate on our nerves, it is also considered normal and displayed in the majority of children. The same behavior, from adults in the workplace, would seem a bit odd.

As the vice president of the media company, I never heard, "Erik, Erik, Erik, Erik, Erik." But the lack of my name being repeated did not mean that my people did not need attention from me and our other leaders. The same children, who so desperately crave attention growing up, eventually become "employees" who join our businesses. There is no denying that everyone in our organization needs proper attention from their colleagues.

According to Forbes, "36% of employees felt so strongly about recognition (or lack of it) that it was the number one reason they're considering switching jobs." Psychology Today states, "The basic human need for attention remains, although sadly, most adults ignore this in both themselves and in others." Just as a seed requires sunlight to unleash its potential and grow into a tree, people require attention to unleash their potential and grow into dynamic team members.

But how much attention is required to ensure that our people feel appreciated for their actions? When I ask people in the workplace to identify things that will make their environments better, "Recognition" is one of the most common answers I hear. I'm guessing that our people might need it more than they are asking for it and more than they are receiving it.

It makes no sense to deprive a seed of sunlight and expect it to fully grow. So, it should make no sense to deprive a person of recognition and expect them to fully grow. In the workplace, we cannot afford to miss the opportunity to unify our people by neglecting the basic human need for attention. It may lead to more conflict.

ATTENTION REDUCES CONFLICT

Psychology Today also adds, "It makes sense that attention and conflict show up in the same paradigm. Challenging issues will naturally arise between two people in any close relationship. However, if a lot of positive attention is bandied back and forth as well, both parties will be more eager to resolve their issues to get back to the good stuff." The level of attention our people receive in the workplace impacts the level of conflict we experience at work.

Attention and conflict are interconnected, and they are either magnified or minimized by how we recognize our people. How important is recognition in the workplace? While there are 24.8 million results for "Workplace Harmony" and 129 million results for "Workplace Conflict," there are 366 million results for "Employee Recognition." Of course, we prefer the term "Team Member," but you get the point.

According to psychologist John M. Gottman, "Attention is not only an essential component for our physical health, it is crucial to all of our closest relationships." If we are truly in the "people" business then the action of recognizing our people cannot be overlooked, especially if we want to build stronger relationships in the workplace. So, let's take a closer look at what *recognition* really means so we can boost it, and experience its powerful effects.

rec · og · ni · tion

noun

- special notice or attention.
- formal acknowledgement of achievement, service, or merit.
- the expression in the form of some token of appreciation.

In the previous chapter, I mentioned that harmonious teamwork is commonplace in the military, in sports, and the movie business but so is recognition. As leaders, we must let our people know their performance, efforts, and results are acknowledged and appreciated.

Sound Bite:
A highly appreciative leader is a highly appreciated leader.

Recognition cannot be an afterthought. People want to know how they are doing. They want to feel valued. It makes sense to acknowledge team members for their achievements, but most businesses do not have a consistent, understood, and inspiring recognition program in place. Although the need is undeniable, most leaders do not know where to start. Let's start with the benefits - why recognition is vital for our people and our success.

THE BENEFITS OF RECOGNITION

In today's ultra-competitive work environment, the winning edge may be our ability to recognize our people more genuine and meaningful than our competition recognizes their people. A strong recognition program has the power to positively enhance nearly every aspect of our businesses. When our people feel acknowledged and appreciated the effect will be felt by our entire team, our leaders, and our customers.

Perhaps the most significant benefit of a well-implemented recognition program is the creation of team members with buy-in; not just happier people. When your team is "all-in," you will achieve greater results in less time. Collapsing time frames for success is reason enough to take action with a recognition program. But there are additional benefits that will flow throughout your workplace environment.

The Key Benefits of Workplace Recognition:

- Accelerate Productivity
- Increase in Profitability
- Enhance Team Morale
- Positively Impact Culture
- Create Collaboration
- Retain Top Talent
- Improve Job Satisfaction

Any one of these benefits should be causing you to flip through the pages of your current recognition program and reevaluate its impact. Now, imagine experiencing all of them. Get in the habit of talking as leaders, dreaming about what would be possible as you achieve higher levels of productivity, morale, and collaboration. Have your dreams turn into realities, and better yet, have them become the norm.

How did we do it? We did not bark orders at our team members to be more productive. We did not issue a memo to be happier. We did not force people to collaborate, which actually hinders collaboration. We experienced these benefits with a simple action - *boosting recognition*.

Remember, your business is like a game of chess – every move counts. Are you ready to make the recognition move?

YOUR BUSINESS IS TO RECOGNIZE

One of the best strategies in chess is to see the game from the vantage point of the person across the table. When it comes to recognizing our people, we need to use the same strategy. By looking at our business from the viewpoint of our team members, the ones who will be substantially impacted by the recognition, we can make each move more meaningful.

Like a game of chess, the key to a unifying recognition program is to determine which move will cause your team members to experience victory – to feel appreciated. One of the foundational principles of recognition is to elicit positive feelings in our people. Gerard C. Eakedale once said that "Recognition is the greatest motivator." Yet, many leaders who seek to have a more-motivated team fail to motivate their people with proper recognition.

Just as a poorly calculated move in chess can cost you the game, a poorly designed recognition program can be just as costly as failing to acknowledge your people at all. Can there be bad recognition? Yes, and before we identify the components of a unifying recognition program, let's first take a look at what could cause some recognition to divide our people.

It can be hard to imagine that recognition can have a negative effect but it is all too common when the types of recognition used are generic and fail to tap into the real needs of the people. Perhaps the most notorious is the Employee of the Month award. While the intentions are good, it is the execution that leaves much to be desired. Recognition should never be a check-the-box item. But many leaders are just looking to get it off their list.

Saying, "Well, I recognized her," is not enough to fulfill the deeper needs of being acknowledged. The Employee of the Month award can quickly lose its luster when it is given, not earned. If the criteria for becoming the Employee of the Month is having your name drawn out of a hat, the team will quickly pick up on the sub-par selection process and move away from their leaders, decreasing productivity in the process.

Sound Bite:
Lackluster recognition can be just as bad as showing no recognition at all, or perhaps worse.

Also, recognition should never be based on the question, "Who do you think we should give it to this month?" Negative feelings can quickly arise when it is known that everyone will have their turn as the "chosen one." When recognition is poorly executed, it is easy for it to lose its real meaning and have the opposite effect. Because recognition is a response to a human feeling, the need for attention, other feelings can also arise, some that we did not expect.

When favoritism is shown and the person being recognized is chosen based on being "liked" by the leader, not by meeting specific criteria, it will soon be followed by jealousy. When one person is rewarded, it's fair to say that others are not. If recognition is not properly created and consistently implemented, feelings can cause team members to do less than what's required. The main objective is that recognition becomes an inherent part of our culture.

CONNECTING RECOGNITION TO YOUR CULTURE

Recognition in the workplace has long been a cornerstone of effective leadership and dynamic results. A well-developed system of acknowledging and rewarding behavior does not look for random things to praise. Instead, a unifying recognition program will pull your entire team together, creating new levels of enthusiasm and cohesion.

In the military, a quick glance at a service member's uniform can tell a lot about his/her military service. We can immediately identify their branch of service. Ribbons are placed, in an order of precedence to display personal accomplishments and unit awards. Service stripes, also known as hash marks, denote years of service. Insignia is placed to acknowledge their rank, and medals identify their rifle and pistol marksmanship awards.

On one uniform, recognition can categorize three elements – personal, unit, and branch. At the media company, I could not issue uniforms, nor could I assign medals and ribbons. But I still wanted to find ways to recognize everyone. I wanted to make people feel worthy and for all of our recognition to be a natural part of our culture.

It doesn't take a rocket scientist to realize that when recognition is meaningful, relevant, and motivating, the possibilities on performance are limitless. Putting it all together may seem like a daunting task, which is why most businesses do little to no unifying recognition, but it is quite simple. Like the military, I identified three categories of recognition - three ways our people could be acknowledged consistently.

Three Categories of Workplace Recognition:

- Personal Recognition
- Team Recognition
- Company Recognition

Personal Recognition:

Everyone appreciates being recognized for exemplary performance or for going the extra mile. Leaders should be aware of the performance of their people, through daily communication and regularly scheduled performance reviews. Recognition that allows the individual to stand out and be congratulated by their peers is critical for maintaining high levels of performance.

- Create forms of recognition that reward **Individual Actions** but is attainable by anyone willing to put in the effort.

Team Recognition:

Not everyone will be your next Michael Jordan, but everyone gets a championship ring on a winning team. Team recognition ensures that people in each department have a chance to be recognized for the overall performance of their team. Create team recognition that is specific to each department, and also roll out the recognition that encourages friendly competition between departments.

- Create forms of recognition that acknowledge **Department Actions** so the whole team can be recognized.

Company Recognition:

One of my favorite reasons for creating a company-wide strategic plan, what we call a Flight Plan, is the ability to share the short-term and long-term goals that help the entire organization to grow and achieve success. When shared goals are reached, we can recognize every single person in the company.

- Create forms of recognition that reward **Total Actions** so the entire team, everyone, can experience recognition for achieving company-wide objectives.

Sound Bite:
Unifying recognition works best when it is seamlessly interwoven into the fabric of your culture.

Recognition needs to be a well-rounded system of personal, team, and company acknowledgments. Just as each wheel of a tricycle is critical to achieving sustainable movement, each category is necessary to move your people with recognition.

CONNECT RECOGNITION TO THEIR NEEDS

Human beings have such a strong desire for positive affirmation in the workplace that even a neutral reaction to our efforts can easily be perceived as a negative one. I've discovered that most businesses struggle with the fundamentals, such as providing performance reviews, so leaders can discuss strengths and weaknesses, successes, and areas for course-corrections.

Scheduling consistent performance reviews is a great place to start. Every team member expects them, and when they fail to happen, it sends a powerful message about how important "people" really are in that culture. At the media company, I relied heavily on well-timed performance reviews to help my people qualify for more recognition.

In most companies, it is not uncommon for the vast amount of memorable recognition and incentives to occur only in the sales department. That makes sense because they are bringing in the sales – the lifeblood of every organization. But remember, to achieve harmony, *Everyone is in Sales.* If your people are not "out" selling, then they are "in" supporting. I have found that the best recognition to support sales should go to the people supporting it – often these are the teams that feel the most overlooked.

At the media company, there was no apparent recognition when I started working there, for any department. Did we have people who did things worthy of recognition? Of course. While there were some "thank you's" (and they were heartfelt) and some lunches (and they were tasty) ordered in for our efforts, we did not have a program to consistently recognize our people. We had nothing identified that they could strive for.

Like me, you may be building your recognition program from scratch. If you already have a reward system in place, then this is a great time to identify the areas it can be stronger. Whether you are creating a new recognition program or enhancing your current one, this is the time to "slow down to speed up."

Taking the time to design a relevant program, one that connects to the needs of our people is paramount. As you put together the recognition program in your company, focus on creating a tool for team empowerment, a tool for effective leadership, and a tool to pull your people together. By keeping three key elements in mind, your recognition program will become part of your culture, unifying your people, and will become a critical component in the *Shared Language of Success*.

Three Elements of a Unifying Recognition Program:

- Ask Questions
- Announce It
- Be Timely

Ask Questions:

When creating or redefining your recognition program, focus on ensuring that each method connects to their needs – do not guess at what means the most to your people. Ask questions from the entire team. Gather information on how they would like to be recognized. Always keep in mind the acronym, WIIFM – What's In It For Me? Your recognition program answers this question, so make sure you get the answer right.

Your team members already know what they want and if you can connect the recognition to their needs and goals, the result can be positive and powerful. Design a simple questionnaire or survey to gain a better understanding of the types of rewards that will move them. Some of their ideas will be expected, some will not. You need to understand both.

Announce It:

According to the article, *The Best Ways to Recognize Employees* by the Business Journal, "A recent Gallup Poll found that almost two out of three people receive no workplace recognition in a given year. This underscores a recent finding from the U.S. Department of Labor that the number one reason people leave their jobs has nothing to do with pay or promotions – they leave because they don't feel appreciated."

While many companies do not have any recognition program, far too many have only a basic form, and I have discovered that most team members do not know it exists. People cannot strive to achieve something if they do not know about it.

As you ask questions about the types of recognition your team would like, you have subtly announced that a recognition program is coming. Keep them posted along the way and make a full announcement as it launches. In the initial implementation phase, leaders should be re-announcing it at team meetings and performance reviews.

Equally important as announcing each form of recognition, be sure to clearly identify and articulate the criteria to earn the recognition. This is critical. Everyone needs to know how to qualify.

Be Timely:

We spend our lives waiting for things. We wait in lines at grocery stores. We wait at red lights. We wait for packages to arrive. There is nothing as frustrating as waiting too long for something. We even wait too long at the doctor's office. But when people are forced to wait to be recognized for their stellar performance, they may lose the desire to receive it if too much time passes.

When we delay recognition, we inadvertently delay high-level performance. Recognition, whether formal or informal, must be timely. We cannot afford to be too "busy" to show our people the attention they earned and deserve.

Sound Bite:
For your recognition program to be impactful, praising your peoples' good work must be timely.

CONNECTING RECOGNITION TO YOUR GOALS

It doesn't matter what industry you're in or what products and services your company sells. If you do not love recognizing the achievements of your people, you are in the wrong position. There really is no greater reward than to recognize your people for their performance and their results. Great leaders love great recognition. We search for ways to recognize our people – consistently!

Your recognition program absolutely needs to connect to the needs of your people. But to be fully effective, you must also connect recognition to the short-term and long-term goals of your company. The outcome of recognition in the workplace is to reinforce the behaviors and activities that deliver better results – supporting and accomplishing the goals of your business.

As my daughter, Erika, once told me, *GOAL* is an acronym: Great Outcome After Leadership. She wrote it on my whiteboard so I could see it each day. The more I saw it the more I realized that she was right. The more leaders recognize their people the more goals they accomplish with them. Connecting recognition to your goals is critical for success.

We have discussed, in great detail, the need for recognition, and we are all on the same page with how important it is. But what recognition should be used? This is a common question that I am asked by most leaders. While recognition can come in many styles, it needs to come from the heart. To truly impact our people for the exceptional work they are doing, all recognition needs to be genuine – authentic.

Because one of the focal points of every business should be to develop cohesive teams, we need to acknowledge and recognize the efforts of teamwork, especially as people come together and work toward shared goals that position us to achieve our vision.

 **Sound Bite:**
Paying attention to our people leads to stronger teamwork.

Business is a team sport and we never win the game by staying on the bench. Teams focus on common objectives – common goals. All the words, speeches, and gestures do little to help our teams to score if they only come from the sideline. To move our people, we need to get on the court and take the shot. Dynamic recognition allows us to take the actions necessary to show the right amount of attention to our team members.

DELIVERING RECOGNITION

Recognition can be delivered in two basic ways: verbally and physically. Verbal recognition is the action of praising someone with our voices. This can be done privately, between you and the team member who earned the recognition, or publicly in front of their peers, at meetings and events. A little praising goes a long way.

Verbal recognition can be expressed by simply saying, "Thank you" or "Great job." Based on the human need for appreciation, I tend to be more specific in saying things like, "I appreciate what you did on that project," or "I want you to know how much I appreciate you." An appropriate pat on the back or firm handshake can add to the feeling created by your verbal appreciation.

Ok, now to the part that causes the most over-thinking – physical recognition. This is the action of doing something to acknowledge and praise people for their good work. But what type of physical recognition is the best to do? Is it monetary? Should you hand out certificates? How about promotions? Physical recognition can come in a wide array of styles. No matter what it looks like, it is a powerful way to elevate appreciation and let your people know your care – more than with words.

Over the years, I have discovered and used numerous forms of physical recognition. While not every type of recognition delivered the results I had hoped for, it is often a matter of continuing to improve it as you go. Below are some of the methods I found to be most successful when *boosting recognition* throughout my entire team.

Types of Physical Recognition:

- Monetary
- Non-Monetary

While both monetary and non-monetary recognition incentivizes our people differently, both are not only necessary for balance, but both are expected by our people. Monetary incentives can be used to reward team members, departments, and the entire company for their efforts. Monetary recognition includes bonuses, cash awards, promotions, stock options, profit-sharing plans, and paid time off. As you may imagine, most people do not have a problem receiving this form of recognition.

While monetary incentives encourage increased performance and some friendly competition between team members, it is not enough to merely "payout" recognition. Non-monetary acknowledgments can often yield a greater result than money when properly delivered. Everything from flexible work hours to certificates can boost recognition. Whatever you choose, make sure it fits the culture of your team.

At the media company, I had a clean slate to work with. Our recognition toolbox was empty. But the owner was not only committed to having me build our program, he was also generous. Like monetary recognition, there is always an investment with any form of non-monetary recognition, too. As with any investment, a return is possible. The greatest return from non-monetary recognition comes after our genuine and sincere delivery.

SELECTING YOUR RECOGNITION

Like Sherlock Holmes, I, and each of our leaders, walked through our facility, looking for clues of elite performance and high levels of teamwork. This tied in with one specific duty in every leader's job description: "Maintain a productive, professional, exciting environment focused on results." The best way to hit our intended results was through a team of people who felt acknowledged, appreciated – recognized.

Our leaders were on a mission, constantly on the lookout for ways to recognize people from other departments, not just members of their own team. When our team members knew that leaders were searching for opportunities to recognize more people, more people sought to be recognized.

Putting thought into your recognition solutions will pay off. We needed each one to be meaningful and moving – unifying our entire team. Everyone understood the recognition that was available to each individual, to the team, and the entire company. They spoke the language of recognition!

One of the easiest and least expensive ways to recognize is to go old school – a handwritten note to show appreciation. Without being too wordy, you can take a typical verbal recognition and write in on a piece of paper or a good old fashioned Post-It Note. You can also compose an e-mail and recognize their achievements. Be sure to "cc" their co-workers to add the extra special touch.

 **Sound Bite:**
Start each day with a message to your team, recognize those who have gone above and beyond the call of duty.

Going back to my military roots, we handed out coins of appreciation to our people for a job well done. In the military, challenge coins are presented, in a handshake, to someone who has exemplified outstanding service. Our coins in the media industry were ordered online and said things like "Great Job" and "Well Done." While far less expensive than military challenge coins, ours provided a sense of accomplishment – they were priceless.

They were only handed out by the owner after leaders informed him of outstanding service during our leadership meetings. The monetary value was low but the impact was high. We began to see people displaying their coins at their workstations. Imagine the impact when a new team member would ask, "What's that?"

I probably discouraged you from the Employee of the Month technique, but we actually used it – properly. Our Team Member of the Month was awarded to the team member who exemplified our culture, teamwork, and commitment to excellence. This person was selected after being discussed each week in our leadership meetings. Leaders were not allowed to nominate someone from their own department, causing each leader to spend time in other departments, looking for clues.

In addition to raising the bar on the selection process, it unified our leaders. They welcomed each other into their departments to witness the performance of their teams. In addition to a coin and a certificate, the Team Member of the Month was presented with a crisp $100 bill. But the key was that it was earned, never given. Tara O'Connor was a star performer who earned it three months in a row!

Boosting recognition was always at the top of my mind. Finding new creative and inspiring ways to show appreciation lit my fire every day. When people performed at top levels, we offered promotions and lateral moves to acknowledge them, which positioned them to hit their goals and ours. For some team members, investing in their professional leadership development or attending sales training was a motivating incentive.

To further sweeten the recognition pot, we added contests specific to each department, such as lowering our error-ratio or increasing positive customer feedback. We did many tours of our facility for potential clients, so the cleanliness of our entire workplace was essential. We created the White Glove Contest and every department eagerly participated.

The team with the most squared away department won the monthly prize – a catered lunch. The winning department had bragging rights and was presented with a crystal trophy to display in their department for the month. It was not uncommon for the winning team to excitedly walk their catered lunch through the other departments before eating it - allowing everyone to smell their victory.

We also allowed people to work from home and provided time-off to people who unselfishly gave more of their time. We made donations to the charity of choice for team members who supported their favorite charity organizations after earning some recognition.

For our sales team, we featured recognition that encouraged everyone to improve each month. Our C.B.E. was a certificate for recognizing their Career Best Effort. Any month that was their highest month, in the history of their career with us, we recognized them in front of their sales peers and leaders from other departments.

We also featured our "% Contest" in sales. We had a one-sheet poster with different prizes, chosen by the sales professional as they had their best month. The payout of prizes started at 10% personal growth, then went to 15%, 20%, and 25%. Each tier featured more lucrative and exciting prizes, all picked by asking questions to our sales team.

But one of my favorite sales recognitions was "Date Night." We valued the extra time our team put into reaching certain milestones. We knew that some of them sacrificed time with their loved ones and we wanted to show how much we appreciated their dedication. Based on qualifying, we sent a limo to pick up the sales professional and their date, taking them to a restaurant of their choice.

As the company hit our key financial goals and accomplished objectives like launching a new service or department, we used these times as milestone markers to recognize the entire team. Because our team positioned us to exceed so many of our goals, we often catered meals for everyone, hosted team picnics, rented bungalows at Malibu Beach for the team and their families, and issued bonuses to the entire crew.

When it comes to recognition, use what works for your people. It should cause team members to strive for it and leaders to look forward to awarding it. Reward the behaviors you want to see duplicated.

Sound Bite:
You should love recognizing your people as much as they love receiving it.

MAKING YOUR MASTERPIECE

By definition, a masterpiece is anything done with masterly skill; an example of excellence. No one starts a business, buys a business, or begins a career to be average. People want to be part of something special and great – a business masterpiece. Each time you recognize your people, that action sets the tone for your final masterpiece – it moves everyone toward the true vision of your organization.

The best performances come from a well-recognized team. This is an action that will always come back to you many times over. A powerful and consistent recognition program allows your people to be part of a movement – *The Communication Movement*.

Disconnected people are a hindrance to the workplace and can drain positive energy from everyone they encounter. When people feel connected, the workplace takes on a completely different vibe – a greater experience. While communication happens every day, it is far too important to leave it to chance.

The Communication Movement is the real focus of leadership. Getting everyone to speak the same language, the *Shared Language of Success* transforms organizations by linking people together with something greater than their job description. It connects people with an unbreakable bond as they harness the unlimited power of their words, speeches, gestures, and actions. Now is the best time to unify your people with all levels of communication.

Communication Catalyst

Recognition Booster

Description: Enhance your current recognition program.

Time of Exercise: 60 minutes

Purpose: To utilize forms of recognition for acknowledging the efforts of your people and unifying them in the process.

Resources: 3x5 cards, pens, whiteboard, whiteboard markers.

Presentation:

- Give a 3x5 card and a pen to each participant.
- Ask participants to list all known forms of recognition currently used in your organization.
- Go around and have each participant share the forms of recognition they listed and write on the white board.
- Next, identify ways to improve your current recognition program to make more people feel appreciated.
- For all forms of recognition, detail the criteria required to earn them.
- Have an open discussion about the impact of your current recognition program and the new forms of recognition that should be included.

Debrief: Once your recognition program has been enhanced, launch it to the entire team, ensuring everyone understands the criteria for being recognized. Leaders should discuss the plan in meetings. Make it known and exciting.

Works Cited

"American Sign Language." *National Institute of Deafness and Other Communication Disorders*, U.S. Department of Health and Human Services, 15 July 2020, www.nidcd.nih.gov/health/american-sign-language.

Blackburn, Kate. "Kate Blackburn, Ph.D." *Kate Blackburn PhD*, 2019, www.kateblackburn.us/2017/10/24/how-long-does-it-take-your-brain-to-process-a-word/.

Dept. of the Army. "Visual Signals TC 3-21.60." *Army Intelligence and Security Doctrine*, 2017, fas.org/irp/doddir/army/tc3-21-60.pdf.

DOD Dictionary of Military and Associated Terms. June 2020, www.jcs.mil/Portals/36/Documents/Doctrine/pubs/dictionary.pdf.

DuBois, Kara. "What Is Verbal Bullying and What Are the Effects of Verbal Bullying - JSY." *Just Say YES*, 11 Nov. 2019, www.justsayyes.org/bullying/verbal-bullying/.

Eakedale, Gerard C. "Recognition Is the Greatest Motivator. - Quote." *AllAuthor*, allauthor.com/quotes/63256/.

Elkins, Katleen. "A Former FBI Hostage Negotiator Says These 2 Words Are Crucial in Any Negotiation." *CNBC*, CNBC, 5 Aug. 2016, www.cnbc.com/2016/08/05/a-former-fbi-hostage-negotiator-says-these-2-words-are-crucial-in-any-negotiation.html.

Harter, Jim. "Historic Drop in Employee Engagement Follows Record Rise." *Gallup.com*, Gallup, 21 Aug. 2020, www.gallup.com/workplace/313313/historic-drop-employee-engagement-follows-record-rise.aspx.

"How Reliable Are Weather Forecasts?" *NOAA SciJinks – All About Weather*, 2020, scijinks.gov/forecast-reliability/.

IATA. "Marshalling Hand Signals (For Aircraft)." *Ground Operations Manual (IGOM)*, 9th ed.

Jarski, Verónica. "10 Things Every Sales Manager Should Know About Sales Performance [Infographic]." *MarketingProfs*, MarketingProfs, 21 Oct. 2013, www.marketingprofs.com/chirp/2013/11909/10-things-every-sales-manager-should-know-about-sales-performance-infographic.

"Lead Paint and Hazards." *HealthLink BC*, 18 Oct. 2019, www.healthlinkbc.ca/healthlinkbc-files/lead-paint-hazards.

Lipman, Victor. "36% Of Employees Say Lack Of Recognition Is Top Reason To Leave Their Job." *Forbes*, Forbes Magazine, 2 Mar. 2019, www.forbes.com/sites/victorlipman/2019/03/01/36-of-employees-say-lack-of-recognition-is-top-reason-to-leave-their-job/.

Marra, Marci. "The Power of Your Words." *Thrive Global*, 16 Oct. 2019, thriveglobal.com/stories/the-power-of-your-words-2/.

"Marriage & Divorce." *American Psychological Association*, American Psychological Association, 2020, www.apa.org/topics/divorce.

Maurer, Robert J. "Why We All Just Need a Little Attention." *Psychology Today*, Sussex Publishers, 18 Nov. 2016, www.psychologytoday.com/us/blog/the-traits-excellence/201611/why-we-all-just-need-little-attention.

Meer, Erin Van Der, et al. "What Body Language Experts Know That We Don't." *Repeller*, 14 Sept. 2020, repeller.com/body-language-expert/.

Miller, Shayne A. "What Is a Vocal Harmony? Learning to Harmonize with Harmony Helper." *Harmony Helper*, 13 Aug. 2020, harmonyhelper.com/2017/10/what-is-a-vocal-harmony/.

Pace, Rachael, et al. "Is a Lack of Trust a Reason for Divorce?" *Divorce Magazine*, 13 Mar. 2019, www.divorcemag.com/articles/ seo-ready-2-12-is-a-lack-of-trust-a-reason-for-divorce.

Pesce, Nicole Lyn. "Stop Saying These Cringeworthy Office Phrases 'ASAP'." *MarketWatch*, MarketWatch, 28 Apr. 2018, www. marketwatch.com/story/stop-saying-these-cringeworthy-office-phrases-asap-2018-04-27.

Rath, Tom. "The Best Ways to Recognize Employees." *Gallup.com*, Gallup, 13 Aug. 2020, news.gallup.com/businessjournal/13888/best-ways-recognize-employees.aspx.

Srivastava, Dr. Ritika. "People Matters." *People Matters Daily Posts Atom*, 2016, www.peoplematters.in/site/interstitial?return_to=%2Farticle%2Femployee-engagement%2Frole-of-communication-in-employee-engagement-14496.

"Types Of Bullying: National Centre Against Bullying." *NCAB*, www.ncab.org.au/bullying-advice/bullying-for-parents/types-of-bullying/.

W., Susie, et al. "How Much Weight Can a Horse Pull? (You'll Be Surprised!)." *Horse Rookie*, 11 Dec. 2019, horserookie.com/how-much-weight-can-a-horse-pull/.

"Weather Forecasting." *ScienceDaily*, ScienceDaily, 2020, www. sciencedaily.com/terms/weather_forecasting.htm.

"What Is the Definition of Hostile Work Environment?" *Job Search*, 2020, www.indeed.com/hire/c/info/hostile-work-environment.

"You Cannot Make Sweet Wine out of Sour Grapes." *StatusMind*, statusmind.com/smart-quotes-2402/.

Acknowledgments

My Deepest Gratitude

This book would never become unified without the support of the following people. I am eternally grateful for the impact you have made in my business, in my life.

Gina, we have used communication to navigate some pretty tough circumstances. You have helped me to strive for greater results, no matter what circumstances we face.

To Erika, my incredibly talented and passionate daughter – you not only sacrificed time with me but you offered GREAT suggestions that made this book better!

To my team, you have each contributed so much to allow me to fill each page with greatness. Saphire, you have posted our communication messages before this book even launched. Sandy, you have embraced our shared language and delivered it to so many people. Jacob, you have again, significantly added to the message of this book, so more people can create movement with their teams.

To my clients, for your desire to create harmony in the workplace, and to unify your people. It has been an incredibly rewarding experience to participate in *The COMMUNICATION Movement* happening in your organizations.

About the Author

Erik Therwanger

Erik Therwanger began his unique career by serving in the U.S. Marine Corps as an air traffic controller. Leadership, honor, and integrity did not end after his four-year tour of duty; they became the foundation of his life, both personally and professionally.

After receiving the news that his wife had been diagnosed with cancer, Erik left his job in the entertainment industry, became her caregiver, and started his new career in sales.

With no formal training, he began selling financial services. Relying on the strategies and techniques he learned as a Marine, he quickly became a top producer, recruiter, and trainer.

Erik returned to the entertainment industry and became the vice president of a media company in Santa Monica, CA. By building leaders, designing their strategic plan, and creating a dynamic sales system, he helped to raise annual sales by over 300%.

Erik's passion for helping others led to the creation of Think GREAT®. He successfully blends his leadership skills, his unparalleled ability to inspire and develop teams, and his wide array of strategic planning and sales experience, to provide practical solutions for individuals and organizations.

The *Three Pillars of Business GREATNESS*™ brings together the concepts from *The LEADERSHIP Connection, ELEVATE,* and *Dynamic Sales Combustion to* provide business leaders, and their teams, with a shared language of *leading, planning,* and *selling.*

Sharing his personal story and elite strategies, Erik's keynote speeches inspire audiences to strive for new levels of greatness. His interactive and powerful workshops highlight his step–by–step process for increasing results.

Erik delivers a compelling message that leaves a lasting impact in organizations, creating the necessary momentum to develop strong leaders, build visionary teams, and *ELEVATE* sales results.

As the author of the Think GREAT® Collection, Erik has combined his challenging life experiences with his goal–setting techniques, to provide proven strategies to enhance the lives of others.

As a trainer and speaker for the spouses of armed services personnel, Erik is deeply aware of their challenges and sacrifices. To help support their education goals, Erik founded the *Think GREAT Foundation,* which is dedicated to awarding scholarships to the MilSpouse community.

For more information, please visit:
www.ThinkGreatFoundation.org

www.ThinkGreat90.com

Please visit our website for more GREAT tools:

- Erik Therwanger's Keynote Speeches
- Workshops and Seminars
- Virtual Training Courses
- Join us at **www.ThinkGREATNow.com**

More life-changing books in

- The LEADERSHIP Connection
- ELEVATE
- Dynamic Sales Combustion
- The GOAL Formula
- The SCALE Factor
- GPS: Goal Planning Strategy
- The Seeds of Success for LEADING
- The Seeds of Success for PLANNING
- The Seeds of Success for SELLING